The Maltese Penguin

For Dorothea who listened to these tales

THE
MALTESE
PENGUIN

FRANK COCKETT

SG BOOKS LONDON

British Library Cataloguing in Publication Data

Cockett, Frank
  The Maltese penguin: stories from the background fog of
  war, 1942–1943.
  1. Malta. Air operations by Great Britain. Royal Air
  Force, 1939–1945 — Biographies
  I. Title
  940.544941092

  ISBN 1–85463–049–0

Typeset by Delatype Ltd, Ellesmere Port, South Wirral
Printed in Great Britain by Whitstable Litho Printers Ltd,
Whitstable, Kent

Published by Smith-Gordon and Company Limited
Number 1, 16 Gunter Grove, London SW10 0UJ, UK.
Telephone: (071) 351 7042

The Siege of Malta
1941 – 1943

The men who fought in the sky over Malta were held in high esteem by the local population: they were greeted wherever they went. People prayed for their safety as the vibrating noise of aero-engines penetrated deep down into the shelters. These daring and gallant pilots fought under conditions which taxed their stamina and morale. Notwithstanding the lapse of over 40 years, Leo Nomis, an American pilot who belonged to 71 Eagle Squadron, UK, and who later served with 229 Squadron operating from Ta'Qali, recalls: ". . . In my opinion, of all the sieges during the Second World War that of Malta was the most famous and unique . . . The stories of the actions at Malta are seemingly endless and, of all my service with the RAF, the memories of those days remain the sharpest and most haunting. Perhaps it was the conditions and the atmosphere which existed in no other theatre of war. There was an aura of fatality about the Malta of those times, which one had to experience to really know. Every pilot I knew, with the exception of the then Sergeant Pilot George 'Screwball' Beurling, cursed his lot and yearned to return to the comparative luxuries of the United Kingdom. But, in retrospect, it was an experience never to be forgotten and always remembered with a certain sense of belonging to history. In short, looking back across the years, serving at Malta, in spite of the hardships, hunger and the constant presence of danger and death, is curiously one of those parts of one's life, which, if given the chance, one would do all over again."

Extract from a letter from Leo Nomis dated 1983

CONTENTS

ACKNOWLEDGEMENTS

The birth of these memoirs owes much to my wife, Dorothea, who insisted on a return visit to Malta after 45 years absence — and encouraged me to write the manuscript, and then read the proofs. A short time before this my stepmother Grace had sent back to me all the original letters which I had written home from Malta in 1942 and 1943. My father had kept them all — neatly in chronological order — among his papers. This archive was a powerful stimulus to my memory.

My thanks also to my children Judy and Richard who read the book in its original form and made helpful and constructive suggestions.

My secretary, Mrs Kate Barber, unflinchingly typed the manuscript, working from my own original scrawly handwriting — no mean feat.

I am grateful to Mr Peter Cotton, the artist who produced the little drawings in the book and also the cover design.

Finally I must thank my publishers who had the courage to take on this somewhat unpromising task.

Frank Cockett

THE MALTESE PENGUIN

INTRODUCTION

I t is generally conceded that the battle of El Alamein, fought and won by General Montgomery and the famous Eighth Army in the desert just west of Alexandria, was the turning point of the last world war, at least as far as Britain was concerned.

Churchill said of it, "Before Alamein we never won a battle, after it we never lost one."

This battle took place between 23 October and 4 November 1942 and resulted in driving Rommel and his Afrika Korps right back to Tripoli and Tunis, leading eventually to the capitulation of all the German forces in North Africa in May 1943.

These campaigns in North Africa were primarily dependent on the outcome of the struggle for control of the supply routes. All the English supplies and troops had to come laboriously round the Cape, then up the Red Sea to Suez, as the Mediterranean was effectively controlled by the Axis powers.

Rommel had a shorter supply route. His supplies—tanks, petrol, men, ammunition, food—came straight across the central Mediterranean from ports such as Genoa and Naples to North African ports such as Tunis, Tripoli, Benghazi and Tobruk. Thus he had a tremendous logistic advantage.

There was only one snag. In the middle of Rommel's supply lines lay the tiny islands of Malta and Gozo. Malta was literally a fortress island with large heavily defended natural harbours and three large airfields. During 1940 and 1941 Malta became an important offensive base for attacking Axis supplies en route to North Africa. Royal Navy surface vessels, submarines and bombers from Malta became a serious nuisance to the enemy and it became increasingly obvious that the Italian forces could not cope effectively.

In December 1941 Hitler and Kesselring (the German commander in the Mediterranean area) decided that this must stop and two whole Flieger Korps (nos. X & XI) of experienced German pilots were established in Sicily with a directive to isolate Malta from all relief by sea and to bomb it into submission. An airborne invasion was also planned.

From that moment on the siege of Malta became deadly serious. For the whole of 1942 the island was subjected to an aerial attack which reduced her capital city and harbours to ruins and nearly succeeded in making her airfields unusable. Moreover, no convoys with relief supplies could get through, so that by September she was nearly starved into submission. The story of how Spitfires were flown into the island from the borrowed American aircraft carrier USS *Wasp*, after the Royal Navy's carriers were sunk, is a matter of history. These Spitfires, in increasing numbers, maintained the defence of the island and gradually won the air battle. Throughout that period of fierce conflict the island's aircraft and submarines maintained their attacks on the enemy supply routes.

All this was made possible only by the arrival of four ships of the celebrated convoy code-named "Pedestal". These battered ships were the survivors of 13 merchantmen who, with a large naval escort, had fought their way through the Mediterranean under almost continuous attack. One of these, the glorious *Ohio*, was a tanker containing the aviation fuel without which the island's fighters could not operate. She arrived in Grand Harbour, Valetta, on 15 August, the day of the feast of Santa Maria. This convoy is still celebrated in story and song on the island, and is known as the "Santa Maria convoy", and its arrival just allowed the island to survive for another three months.

However, by October 1942 the island was so short of food and all other supplies that its surrender was imminent. It was saved in the nick of time by the victory at El Alamein.

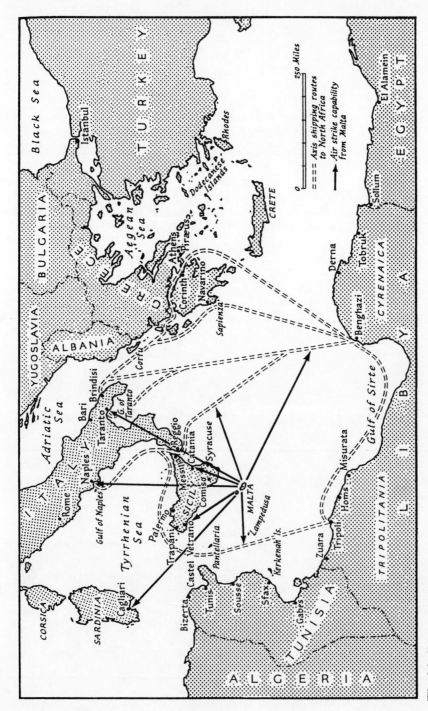

The Mediterranean just before the battle of El Alamein, showing how the Maltese Islands lay right across Rommel's supply lines

It was in September 1942 that I arrived in Cairo after a long passage round the Cape, lasting about six weeks, in a large troop convoy. A day later I was in a transit camp under canvas just outside Cairo, waiting to know my fate. There was a general air of expectancy in the camp as the "buzz" had got through that something special was afoot in the desert. Everybody was hoping to go there. But Malta at that time was considered by us a lost cause. For pilots a posting to Malta was regarded pretty much as a death sentence. Ordinary ground personnel, if they survived, expected to end up fairly soon as prisoners of war.

It was, therefore, with a marked sinking feeling that I scanned my posting chit a few days later—Malta!

I had qualified as a doctor at St Thomas' Hospital, London, just at the outbreak of war in 1939. As a house surgeon there in 1940 and 1941 I had been a very minor member of a team which helped succour the casualties of the first London blitz. I was no stranger to being bombed, as I had actually been in St Thomas' when it received its first two major direct hits on 9 and 13 September 1940. I must be one of the few people still alive who stood on one of the high balconies of St Thomas' Hospital and looked across at the dome of St Paul's Cathedral, miraculously untouched but lit up and ringed by fire as the city around it blazed on the night of 10 May 1941.

After the London blitz in early 1941 I did a job as resident surgical officer at a Guildford hospital and so obtained quite a reasonable surgical experience. It was, in fact, at this time that I determined to make surgery my career. However, as the war seemed to be taking a turn for the worse in early 1942, I decided that perhaps I should volunteer for one of the armed forces. I chose the navy, but they informed me that they had enough medicos, so I opted for the RAF. This turned out to be a happy choice!

~~~~~~~~~~~~~~~~~~~

Many distinguished people have written their war memoirs. Admirals, generals, air marshals, and politicians have published their various books about the epochal struggle which was the last world war. These are important documents and a matter of "history".

In addition, many of the fighting men who lived to tell the tale have done so in books that thrill and excite us. As we read these stories of fighter pilots, destroyer commanders, special service operations and such like, we are overcome with awe and admiration for these supermen and heroes. They really have got a story to tell and most of them tell it extremely well.

These memoirs, however, are different.

This is a story of a distinctly unheroic young newly qualified doctor who, after a week's course on how to be an RAF officer, was flown into the battle of Malta at the height of the famous siege, in October 1942.

Altogether, I spent a year on Malta and Gozo during the period of the end of the siege to the invasion of Sicily. I was lucky enough to be closely involved on Gozo with one of the little "sideshows" of the Sicily invasion. This was an episode of dream-like quality which has, as far as I know, never been recorded before—except as a short passing paragraph of the official history. After the invasion forces had moved on to Sicily and Italy I saw the transition of Malta and Gozo from being the centre of the world stage to—once more—a sleepy forgotten pair of islands.

The impressions of that never-to-be-forgotten year were etched indelibly on my fresh young mind. They are as clear today as they were 47 odd years ago.

During the post-war years, when I was busy making a career in surgery, I formed the habit of writing little jottings and essays about those times. They were still so vivid in my memory that I found myself writing them in the present tense—almost as if I was still there. This format has been retained in this book.

These essays record the day-to-day emotions and impressions of an extremely unimportant person who found himself suddenly, through no fault of his own, in the middle of great events, a feather blown to and fro by the winds of war. I think I can truthfully say that my activities during that year went entirely unnoticed, and in no way either contributed to or hindered the war effort by one jot or tittle.

However, although unheroic myself, I did have the rare

privilege of living at close quarters with some people who were heroes in every sense of the word.

These included the Fleet Air Arm pilots based at the airfield of Hal Far, who flew their slow old torpedo-carrying Albacore aircraft on dangerous missions night after night, attacking the Axis shipping supply lines. Their activities, together with the submarines based on Malta, and the torpedo-carrying Beauforts, were the main reason why Malta was such a thorn in Rommel's side during the desert war.

Indirectly, therefore, they were partly responsible for the ferocious air bombing attacks on Malta, which Hitler mounted in order to "neutralize" the island.

These aviators were mostly young volunteer civilians from every walk of life, who had been hastily trained, as either pilots or observers, and then thrown into the conflict. Their losses were high, and the strain under which they operated was considerable. I was lost in admiration for the extraordinary courage of these very ordinary young men, plucked from a safe civilian existence, and now engaging in this very stressful and nerve-racking type of air warfare.

Someone once wrote that war is 90 per cent boredom, punctuated by 10 per cent terror. This is certainly true. There are also elements of the unexpected and even sometimes of the ridiculous, as anyone who reads this account will quickly appreciate.

Everyone was living under stress of one sort or another, not least the Maltese themselves. The year I spent there taught me a lot about the reactions of my fellow men in all sorts of extreme circumstances, and it also gave me a new sympathy and understanding. Oddly enough, boredom and lack of occupation was often just as potent in breaking up a man's character as was the more obvious stress of being in daily danger of losing one's life.

War is like a great big stew, it mixes people of unlikely backgrounds together and stirs them up. As a doctor (or, indeed, any other professional man) one's essential contacts and friends tend to be other people in the same line of business and, therefore, one acquires a rather restricted and cushioned view of life. One year in Malta during those eventful times was a powerful antidote

19

to this, and I certainly emerged from it a wiser and perhaps a more complete person.

The essays that follow may appear a little disjointed, having been written at different times, but they do form a series in chronological order.

I dedicate them, respectfully, to the Fleet Air Arm pilots and observers of 826, 827 and 828 Squadrons, who were so kind to me!

CHAPTER 1

NIGHT FLIGHT TO MALTA

"... a rather used up looking old DC3 ..."

ONE

Night Flight to Malta
October 1942

It is dark, and it's cold, and it is half an hour before dawn. I am walking up a rough path from the wretched little village of Birzebuggia to the RAF station at Hal Far. I am all alone, the rest of the island is asleep apart from the routine night watches. It is very eerie, not to say actually frightening. Every so often my foot dislodges a stone and a startled goat in the dark croaks m-a-a-a-which startles me more than the goat, and my pulse leaps up to about a hundred.

What the hell am I doing here? Well . . . it's October 1942 and it's Malta and we are just nearing the end of the battle of Malta.

You see, the Air Ministry decided that Malta needed three more doctors. They could not get enough food to the island, but three more doctors—OK?

After getting into the RAF as a doctor, rather a newly qualified one, they sent me all the way round the Cape in a closely guarded convoy, to end up in a transit camp in Cairo. Here, under canvas in a bit of the desert, we exist for about ten days. It's very hot by day and very cold by night.

Then it comes without any warning, our posting! Three doctors for Malta—you, you and you.

Malta, if you please, hundreds of miles behind enemy lines

at El Alamein. How do they expect us to get there? Submarine, or something? Not a bit of it. Just report to the airfield with your posting chit and one small suitcase this evening. And there it was, a rather used-up looking old DC3.

The pilot strolls up to us. "You the docs?" he says, "OK well climb in."

No parachutes or any of that nonsense. It's just us, one or two other guys, and a lot of packing cases and large oddly shaped parcels wrapped in sacking—stores for beleaguered Malta.

We are really frightened, three very frightened doctors!

We're sure to be shot down by some prowling night fighter in this slow old machine. And even if we do get there we won't be able to land because we've heard that the Malta airfields are just a mass of bomb craters.

The pilot, however, is very cool, not to say a trifle bored with all this routine business. He is quite young and has a rather academic air which a faded old tunic and shorts and moustache cannot quite hide. My guess is that he was a master at a public school before all this, or maybe a young Cambridge don.

Somehow his matter-of-fact air, as he potters around seeing to a few last minute things, rubs off on to us a little. Only a little though, we are very quiet.

My two companions have prepared themselves for this journey with large doses of whisky which have left them in a zombie-like state. I confess that I too have had a tot. I have also given the matter of "what to do if shot down over the sea" considerable thought. My plan depends on the fact that my suitcase is a very stout, hard-backed affair and very light as well. Indeed, it has already survived considerable punishment. On the first warning that we are going to ditch I will rapidly open the suitcase, empty it and close it again, and then tie it to myself with my raincoat belt. It will be my own private dinghy, a large air bubble inside hard leather. Rather like a coracle, only better, or so I reason. I put a bottle of water and a case of biscuits in the suitcase as rations.

Such careful planning makes the last rather tense hour or so, while we are in purdah waiting to board, pass much more quickly. It is surprising what a morale booster just having a plan is, even a crack-pot one like this.

Just before take off the co-pilot picks his way along to us between the packages, with three Mae Wests. "You can wear these if you like", he says, "we'll be flying low over the water most of the way."

What joy! With tremendous lightening of my anxiety I buckle this delightful piece of apparatus on. Normally only operational pilots are supposed to wear these, and at this time of the war, after the Battle of Britain, the Mae West is a sort of status symbol for the fighter pilots. I have never worn one before and suddenly feel much better about the whole business.

At this point the pilot, whom we can just see sitting up front beyond the packages, says something rather brief to the control tower, opens the throttles, swings the aircraft round, and taxis for about ten seconds and then with a roar, takes off.

As we leave the little desert airfield just outside Cairo blackness engulfs the three passengers. Night is falling rapidly and we are ranged along the side of the aircraft on a narrow metal seat, just part of the cargo. No windows. No lights. I can just make out a very dim glow in the nose of the aircraft where the pilot is, which I suppose is the compass light.

We settle down and the engine noise drones on steadily. My two companions appear to be either asleep or unconscious, but I am only too wide awake.

After about 20 minutes the aircraft makes a turn and seems to be coming down. I am frozen to my seat and my pulse races. This is it. Probably a night fighter!

However, we level out and drone on again. I remain frozen upright on my little hard bench, and apart from repeated examinations of the door opening mechanism, which I can just make out in the dark as my eyes are now accommodated to night vision, I remain in this position scarcely moving during the whole flight.

After what seems hours the co-pilot suddenly appears. "You all right?" he enquires. I grunt a sort of affirmative. "We've just arrived," he says, "but we've got to stooge around a bit; there's an air raid on." Then he stumbles up front again.

We all feel suddenly immensely relieved that we are there—air raid or no air raid.

Well, we stooge around for a bit and then the aeroplane suddenly seems to become more purposeful, flies straight for a bit and suddenly there's a slight jolt and we are down.

My God! *We've made it.* Relief pours over me like a flood: I can't believe it. We taxi over what is obviously some pretty rough ground and come to a halt.

The co-pilot comes down and opens the door in the side of the plane without a word. Outside it is still dark, although dawn is not far away. Shadowy figures push some mobile steps up to the door and we descend clutching our suitcases. It's cold and unwelcoming. Everybody is very silent or mono-syllabic when words are required.

As we are led off, I turn and look back. I can just see the pilot who has his head down checking something in the nose of the aeroplane. He doesn't even look up at us or wave or anything. We are just another lot of baggage for Malta as far as he is concerned.

I look at the aeroplane, a rather clapped out looking DC3. No lights, no glamour, just an awkward shadowy shape and they are already unloading the packing cases. No matter—to me the old DC3 will always be the most beautiful aeroplane in the world.

〰〰〰〰〰〰〰〰〰

Transport command ran a supply flight to Malta from Cairo three times a week using American DC3s. These supply flights ran regularly throughout the difficult days of the siege of Malta, right up to and just after the battle of El Alamein. Throughout this period not a single aircraft, or man, or package was lost on these long night flights.

Of course, nobody told me this until long after the war!

CHAPTER 2

ARRIVAL IN MALTA AND STARVATION

"... the bomb falls on an aircraft pen, about fifty yards away ..."

TWO

ARRIVAL IN MALTA AND STARVATION
OCTOBER 1942

So, I've actually arrived in fabulous Malta. We've heard so much about it, the relentless Italian and German mass bombing, the air battles, the Malta convoys, the starvation. This is certainly where the action is anyway. It is better than ruddy old balloon command back home, which was just like being a back room clerk while all the world was at war just outside your windows.

I pick my way from the aircraft towards a shelter, which I can just make out in the cold dawn light. All around are bomb craters, some partly filled in. It looks like the surface of the moon. We are led down some steps into a room with a long table and benches.

Somebody hands us a small chit and on this is written "operational meal". We sit down at the table. After a while a Maltese steward appears and places before each of us one piece of white bread lightly buttered, two wholemeal biscuits and one slice of corned beef. By this time I have a nasty headache and I am feeling slightly sick. Fortunately, accompanying this incongruous mixture is a hot cocoa which is just what I need.

At this moment we are joined by a pilot and his observer. They have just come in from a Beaufort torpedo bomber patrol. They have one of these operational meal chits. But when their meal comes, behold, the corned beef is surmounted by a genuine but very small poached egg. They take absolutely no notice of us newcomers and eat in silence. I am still feeling sick and headachy so I push my plate away without touching the unappetizing morsel on it.

This simple act creates an immediate sensation.

The two air-crew stop dead in mid-mastication. After an electric pause, the pilot addresses me.

"Are you going to eat that?", he says.

I say "No."

"Do you mind if we have it?", he says.

He takes my plate, the corned beef is divided exactly in half, as is the slice of bread. The half piece of bread and the half corned beef, plus one wholemeal biscuit, are transferred to the plate of his observer, and silence descends once again.

Well, I knew Malta is starving, but this little scene on my arrival drives it home in no uncertain manner.

Little do I know that within a week I shall be in a similar state to those two pilots!

After this we are hustled off in a battered old jeep. The other two doctors are off-loaded somewhere in Valetta, but I am taken straight out to an airfield called Hal Far, quite a long way out on a corner of the island, which is to be my home for a bit. The roads are appalling, with lots of pot holes and bomb craters here and there. So it is quite an exciting drive just as dawn is breaking.

My arrival at Hal Far is certainly dramatic enough for anyone. No sooner has the jeep dumped me outside this battered and bomb-scarred ruin of a building, which is apparently the station sick quarters, than a German ME 109 fighter bomber comes screaming in making a surprise attack in the dawn light! There is a tremendous cr-r-r-ump as the bomb falls on an aircraft pen about 50 yards away. We all fall flat on our faces and I put my suitcase over my head for protection. After a minute everybody gets up again and carries on normally. Apparently this is pretty routine stuff!

The ME 109s, which are really fighter aircraft, have been fitted to carry a couple of bombs. They fly low over the water to escape the radar, and then pop up over the cliffs. Usually they effect complete surprise. Such attacks are called "sneak" raids, or "hit and run" raids.

I go into the front room of sick quarters and a medical orderly appears and offers me a cup of tea. As I feel tired and groggy and have a headache this is very acceptable.

Soon the station medical officer appears and we have a short talk, but it is not very successful as, (a) I am not in the mood for a chat and, (b) he is not expecting me. He packs me off, with my faithful brown leather case, down to the nearby village of Birzebuggia where I am allotted a cold little bare room with a bed in it. I am told to wait in the officers' mess, a small and modestly furnished house on the waterfront which has been temporarily taken over. Here I am eventually discovered by the quarter-master, who is gruff but not unfriendly.

He takes me to his "office", another small barely furnished room in another little house. We have an important interview about rations, as he is in charge of all stores. My week's ration of butter, and sugar, and tea, is doled out from three tins. A packet of wholemeal biscuits is handed over. I look at this miniscule collection in some surprise and with some foreboding. The truth is that I would normally get through this lot in a couple of days!

Meals consist of bread, oatmeal biscuits, and corned beef in very small quantities. Just occasionally an apple or small orange appears. Twice a week we have a small egg for breakfast.

The cooks do wonders with corned beef. Sometimes it is hot, sometimes cold; it is stewed, minced (corned beef cottage pie is achieved by four people pooling their rations for a day), devilled, fried and in general gets every possible treatment in the cooks' repertoire.

After one week I am in a state of chronic hunger, and am beginning to lose weight, and this gets slowly and steadily worse.

Even more impressive than the physical effects of hunger are the mental effects.

The most notable thing is that one thinks about food most of the day. As a normal healthy young chap I don't remember giving the question of food practically any thought at all outside meal times.

For all my life up to now, an appetizing and varied diet has been regularly placed before me by various agencies, such as my mother, and later St Thomas' Hospital Students' Club, and later still by various hospitals and the RAF. I don't believe I have ever given all this more than a passing thought.

But now, to my intense surprise, my subconscious mind conjures up long forgotten dishes in lurid detail practically whenever I am unoccupied (which is most of the time). A recurring and most vivid apparition is baked jam roll, a favourite second course at the Students' Club at threepence a go. Another one is a particularly delicious sticky ginger pudding which my mother used to make and which I have not thought of for years. I wake up with blackberry and apple tart, and go to sleep with bread and butter pudding. The interesting thing is that I never seem to dream of roast beef or steak, it is always puddings of some sort. I suppose perhaps the corned beef keeps the meat apparitions at bay!

The great thing is if you have a friend in the navy, because at this time convoys are just beginning to arrive in Malta after a lot of hard fighting on the way. After about a month I hear that a destroyer is coming in as part of a convoy escort, in which a friend of mine is a surgeon lieutenant—L.R.S. Taylor, of the Hunt class destroyer HMS *Aldenham*.

Now we all know that the navy has a hard time—but one thing they are not is hungry. Their ships are stocked with good things to eat and drink, as well as more war-like stores. So I wangle special leave that evening to go down to Grand Harbour to see my friend and after an eventful evening playing a deadly serious game of Monopoly in the ward room, come away with my prize—a large tin of marmalade!

This makes me top dog in the mess for nearly a whole week.

It comes about in the following way. After two months or so of oatmeal biscuits as the main article of diet everybody is heartily sick of them, and as a variant a concoction called biscuit pudding is born. This needs a syndicate of five or six to pool their biscuit ration for one or even two days. The biscuits are pounded up in a mortar very thoroughly by hand to make a passable imitation of rather brown flour. A little of our precious butter ration and a little sugar is pounded into the mixture and then a bit of water to make it "gooey". Finally comes the free-for-all phase of the cooking when members of the syndicate throw in any scraps which they have been able to scrounge during the day. Orange peel, grapes and an odd date or two all get stirred in at this stage. Then the concoction is baked.

The result is a somewhat stodgy baked pudding, but a wonderful change from our dull daily rations. However, with a fairly generous topping of marmalade it becomes a dish such as has not been seen in the mess for many months.

Our syndicate is watched by many envious eyes, and in fact an ugly scene is only just avoided by strategic doling out of small amounts of marmalade to the opposition.

Soon after this, convoys begin to arrive in Malta with increasing frequency, and the rations improve rapidly.

Three months or so of existence on a very inadequate diet, however, is a most instructive experience in the surprising and variable ways in which one reacts to this particular form of stress. In future I, for one, will always regard my meals, and the art and science of preparing them, with due reverence!

CHAPTER 3

A PENGUIN AT WAR

A penguin is a flightless bird. During the last world war non-flying officers were often referred to as penguins. Although considered one of the lower forms of life during wartime, even they have reactions and emotions!

THREE

A Penguin at War

I have been here in Malta now for two whole weeks, right in the centre of the action, so to speak, and the fact of the matter is, that I can't find anything to do! They ship me round the Cape to Suez, and then fly me here at vast expense and no little risk, so they must want me here for some reason—but I just can't discover it!

The airfield and RAF station is at Hal Far, up on the cliff; but the mess and all the officers and men are billeted in the little seaside village of Birzebuggia, which is about a mile away. The reason for this is "dispersal". The airfield gets bombed and strafed so much in the air raids that nobody but essential operational personnel are allowed to sleep up there. This means I have to get up at about 5 a.m. and trek up to the airfield, to be on hand for dawn operations.

It is a cold and dismal solitary walk, and after a fortnight of it I am really fed up. Dawn and dusk are the favourite times for raids and fighter patrols and such like and I (being the junior) have to be on hand in the control tower near the "blood wagon" when the Spitfires take off or land.

So far nothing dramatic has happened up there. The pilots, if they do get back, are so good that they usually land their machines without trouble, even when damaged. When the place is bombed or strafed everybody is so quick and practised at taking cover that there have been no serious casualties.

I'm such a new boy straight out from England, and a mere doctor at that, that nobody really wants to talk to me at all. Everybody here has been in the thick of the rather grim battle of Malta for so long, and are so busy with the war, that I am just a bit of a nuisance into the bargain.

There is a whole fighter squadron on this station, but so far I haven't met a single pilot in the mess. I just don't know where they get to. They seem to live a totally separate life.

So far I've exchanged a few words with the quartermaster (about rations) and with the intelligence officer, but of course he is inhibited because of security. The only fellow citizen is my senior medical officer who is a flight lieutenant, but I don't even get to see him that much. He has been here a long time and is a bit "bomb happy". He has managed to run sick-quarters for a year in a bombed out corner of the old RAF building, and has managed to stay alive all this time during which he has been bombed continuously and starved into the bargain. He also regards me as a bit unnecessary.

The worst moment is when I actually run into the wing commander (Wg Cdr David Douglas Hamilton) in the control tower. They call it the control tower, actually it is a sort of raised dug-out heavily sand-bagged and concreted against blast. It is just high enough to get a clear view of the runway. Well, I go in after my usual dawn walk up from the mess at Birzebuggia and there he is standing silent, back in the shadows.

He is a small fair man with a little droopy moustache. He is dressed in shorts and tunic and his cap is pushed slightly back on his head. On his left chest is the ribbon of the DFC and bar. He is one of the select band of Malta fighter pilots who has led the squadron through the thick of the battles, and he comes of an old and well known titled family. I am totally overcome with awe. He is a wing commander so I think I had better salute, and I do so as instructed at the School for Officers. He looks straight through me and I don't believe I register at all—except as another useless body. I remain petrified in my corner of the dug-out until he suddenly leaves without a word.

Time goes on and I get to know a few of the pilots, but I never lose that feeling of entering a privileged private world of these men at the sharp end who are actually doing the fighting.

A few days later I find a new young pilot drooping about in our run-down mess. He is a new boy and doesn't know where things are, so I show him. He actually talks to me and tells me his name. This is the first break in the rather grim atmosphere and I feel quite elated.

I don't see him again and after a week or so I see another pilot briefly and summon up courage to ask about pilot officer so-and-so.

"Is he about?", I ask rather off-hand?

"No", comes the reply, "he went in last Friday."

"How do you mean, 'went in'?" I ask.

The other pilot eyes me with distaste and simply says, "We were on a low level sweep over the sea, and he just went in." End of conversation.

It transpires that this sometimes happens to new pilots. The squadron flies low over the sea to Sicily, to get below the radar beam, and thus achieve a surprise attack on the enemy airfields. Flying a Spitfire at an altitude of 20 to 30 feet above the sea for a whole 20 or 30 minutes requires intense concentration and complete immobility. You only have to lean forward a bit, or scratch your nose or something, and this alters the trim of the aircraft and in she goes, all in a split second.

This was what happened to my new-found friend. I mourn him—no one else does—he was my only friend and gloom descends on me for a day or two. What a bloody waste.

One day about this time I am sitting on the balcony of the bombed-out stone mess building on the station, it is mid-morning and suddenly there is an air raid . . . high level bombers. The Malta anti-aircraft barrage goes into action and in no time at all the paved square between me and the control tower is full of fragments of falling shrapnel. You can hear them "pinging" through the air and falling with a high pitched crack on the paving stones of the square. Very unhealthy! The trouble is that I really ought to be in the control tower in case they start putting up some of our Spitfires.

The problem is how to get across the square as I have no tin hat. If I run, the chaps on the control tower might see me and I would be the laughing stock of the place in no time. So now is the time to show a little courage, I say to myself. You have got to walk across this open area slowly and normally. So I do it—it's quite hard to stop myself from running in sheer panic—as there is quite a shower of shrapnel and there are quite a number of little "zings" in the air as I progress.

It takes me about four minutes to get to the control tower, where lo and behold they are all wearing tin hats—and they actually give me one!

This little private exercise makes me feel a bit better and more able to face living amongst pilots who often face death several times a day.

The trouble is that these fighter pilots fly single-seater machines. There is no way that I can go up with them and share their experience in even a small way.

After about a month of this sort of existence things seem to quieten down a little. There are fewer raids and I am allowed to live in the old married quarters buildings up on the perimeter of the airfield, and some semblance of an officers' mess is set up in another of the old bomb-damaged buildings.

I actually start to meet a few of the pilots off duty and get to know them a little better.

I must say that many of them are really outstanding characters. The fact of the matter is that to be a successful fighter pilot and survive in Malta, you have to be well above average both mentally and physically. Most of them are very alert and intensely individual people, who would, I think, quickly rise to the top of any walk of life in peace-time.

Flight Lieutenant Atkinson, for example, is an ex-Battle of Britain pilot, badly burned on face and hands after a crash early on in the war. He spent about a year in the hands of the plastic surgeons, and his face is just a terrible-looking travesty of what a face should be like. Yet out of this face comes a pleasant quiet cultured voice, and you don't have to be with him for very long to realize that here is a man of an exceptionally firm and stable temperament. Nothing is going to upset him or deflect him from his purpose. He came back from an intruder mission over Sicily the other day, and on arrival over the airfield informs control in a very matter-of-fact voice that he is "a bit shot up" and that his "undercart (wheels) is stuck up". He then proceeds to fly round the airfield for about ten minutes until his tank is dry. Then he tells control that he is coming in for a belly landing at the side of the runway (so as not to muck up the runway for any other planes landing or taking off—very thoughtful of him!). At about two thousand feet he switches off the engine and comes in like a glider to make a perfect belly landing just where he said he would.

I have had plenty of warning so I am on the spot in the fire tender as he comes to a shuddering halt in a cloud of dust. In a leisurely manner he climbs out and surveys the machine, which is pretty well intact except for a bent propellor.

"Hullo, doc", he says, "got a cigarette?"

I hand him my packet and the matches. His hand is rock steady, and he is as cool as a cucumber. What a man!

He is definitely my favourite pilot, partly because he has spent so much time in the hands of the medical profession. He is quite used to doctors and he chats away to me in a completely uninhibited manner, whenever I meet him.

Another amazing character is Wing Commander Adrian Warburton DSO, DFC and bar who is, of course, a legend on the island. He has been here on and off all through the past two years doing PRU flights (PRU = photographic reconnaisance unit). He flies stripped out Beaufighters and, more recently, a stripped down Spitfire and regularly penetrates deep into enemy territory to get information about shipping and troop movements. Apparently, his photographs never need magnification to see what is there because he takes them from about 50 to 100 feet, and the required information is there for all to see—just as in a home snapshot. He then comes home pursued by hordes of ME 109s, which he somehow manages to shake off. He is absolutely a law unto himself and subscribes to no known RAF discipline or any other typle of discipline.

One evening he turns up in the mess. This is rather a rarity in itself as he usually does not come near the place. I am introduced as the local doc. I must admit that I find him a most alarming character. He is strikingly good looking, with a mop of blond hair, but it is his piercing blue eyes which get you! They look right into you and through you, and send a slight chill up and down your spine. His devil-may-care attitude is enhanced by his dress, which is anything but regulation RAF namely, battledress top with open-neck shirt and silk scarf instead of a tie; also corduroy trousers and, on top of it all, he is wearing his hat—which is rather old and dirty—in the mess. They call him "Warbie", but it is obvious that everybody is slightly in awe of him and there is a distinct aura of unease in the mess whilst he is there.

The reason why he is there is that his second in command, a flight lieutenant with an enormous handlebar moustache and pop-eyes, is going to play the mess piano for a bit. He was, apparently, a cabaret performer before the war, and looks like it. He plays the piano very well and livens things up a bit with some racy songs. But, as soon as he has finished, "Warbie" gets up and goes. Actually, this flight lieutenant is very nearly as harum scarum as his master. His job is to fly an old Walrus amphibian aircraft out to sea when his master is on a mission, to be on hand to pick him up if he has to ditch his Spitfire. One day as he is bringing the Walrus in to land at Hal Far he simply does a belly landing without lowering his wheels. Fortunately, the Walrus is a very strong aircraft and little damage is done, except to make a large furrow on the runway.

He climbs out of the aircraft and roaring with laughter tells me that he simply forgot to lower the undercarriage. He thinks this is a tremendous joke. He really is quite mad and irresponsible, but I gather this is just the sort of colleague that Warburton likes. He doesn't go for ordinary straight-forward sensible pilots.

On another day, as I am collecting some stores from Bigi Hospital, I am allowed into the main fighter control room which is in a tunnel hewn out of the solid rock, close to Grand Harbour in Valetta. It is difficult to imagine a more secure place! Here, deep in the rock, the fighter controllers run the battle of Malta. They play an endless game of chess, day in, day out, in which the white pieces are the Germans and Italians, and the stakes are life and death. The pieces are all laid out on a large table in the centre of the room, on which is arranged a large map of Sicily, Italy, Malta and North Africa.

Several girls round the table act as croupiers and move the pieces to their places as a battle develops. The walls are plastered with information about the various squadrons, their state of readiness and so on. The fighter controller sits on a balcony overlooking the whole set-up, and he has a radio telephone with which he is in touch with all the pilots and stations. You can't hear what he says to them, but the pilots' replies come over the amplifier loud and clear.

While I am there a minor crisis is developing, as the radar has just shown a large plot developing over one of the Sicilian airfields.

The controller is busy bringing some of our squadrons to readiness and has just scrambled two sections into the air. He is busy giving course and height to the pilots, and you can hear their laconic replies over the loud speaker. It's all in the specialized jargon of the ops room—"angels" is the word for altitude, "vector" is direction, "tally-ho" is a direct sighting. The pilots' voices from the planes in the air, who are being "vectored" onto the Sicilian plot, are very clear, you can even tell the nationality of the pilots. One voice which is particularly clear is unmistakably Australian and another sounds South African. The controller seems to know them all personally. There is a moment of excitement as one of them says "tally-ho" but then things seem to fizzle out a bit as the "plot" disperses and does not approach Malta.

It is really impressive how efficient and quick the whole thing is, but it must be very wearing doing this 24 hours a day, every day, for two years—which is what this ops room has done. Apparently, Air Vice Marshall Park, who was one of the great pioneers of the fighter control system in the Battle of Britain, put the final polish on it when he became AOC Malta, and it is now the most efficient thing of its kind in existence, and I can well believe it, having seen it in action. The other name which everybody speaks of with reverence is the chief fighter controller, Group Captain Woodhall who was here even before Park. What he doesn't know about air fighting around Malta is not worth knowing!

As I am living now most of the time up on the airfield itself, I mostly use a second officers' mess, which has now been set up in an old bombed building quite near the control tower. It is here that the Fleet Air Arm pilots have their quarters and generally congregate. They are a whole new experience.

CHAPTER 4

THE FLEET AIR ARM AT HAL FAR

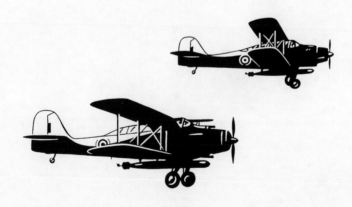

Torpedo-carrying Albacores in flight.

FOUR

THE FLEET AIR ARM AT HAL FAR

The Fleet Air Arm has been operating from Hal Far for about two years. They have very awkward and ungainly looking aeroplanes called Albacores. These are two-seater biplanes and underneath the cockpit, between the wheels, they carry a large torpedo.

They go out at night in search of enemy shipping bound for North Africa full of stores, or ammunition, or troops for Rommel. They operate either alone or sometimes in twos or threes. It's a lonely and nerve-racking job, not just because of the danger of attacking well-armed ships, but also because of the worry of getting back to the tiny island of Malta at night, after a two or three hour patrol with petrol running low. The pilots, therefore, depend a greal deal on their observer, who sits in the rear cockpit and who has to be a fine and accurate navigator.

From my point of view this rear cockpit is an absolute godsend because it means that sometimes I can go up with the pilots on flight tests or exercises. Once I have done this several times, I find myself suddenly accepted by The Fleet Air Arm pilots and rapidly get to know them and make friends.

For me the great breakthrough comes when some units of the fleet are nearby and a dummy "altitude attack" on them is planned. I am allowed to go on this as observer to the leading pilot, with the job of getting some photographs of the attack.

The idea is that the squadron approaches the target at a great height (about 8000 feet) and then when in position, each aeroplane, one after the other, puts its nose down in a near vertical dive. Then you are supposed to pull out of the dive at about 100 feet or so above the water, drop your torpedo very near the ship you are attacking and then fly on right over the ship as there is no time to turn away, jinking and turning to escape the anti-aircraft fire. I must say I thought the whole performance needed a lot of nerve, let alone skill, even when the whole thing was just a practice.

Anyway, I take my place in the rear cockpit—all kitted up with parachute, Mae West, goggles, the lot—and duly take some good aerial photographs. Then my pilot says over the intercom "OK, we're going into the dive now" and puts the nose of the plane vertically down. Well, the first ten seconds or so are all right but, then as our speed increases alarmingly, so does my feeling of rising panic. I think, my God, I hope he knows what he is doing, as we approach the water head on, but at that moment my pilot pulls out of the dive violently and suddenly. For the first time I feel the full effects of "g". I almost black out completely, but before I actually lose consciousness I feel my feet pressing hard on the floor, my stomach falling out and my facial skin being pulled down—a truly weird sensation. Even more embarrassing, all my nasal secretions are pulled out of my nose onto my knees!

I come to after two or three seconds to find the aeroplane almost directly over a large cruiser and just about to collide with the mast. We avoid this and then do some more aerobatics for good measure.

Apparently the exercise was a huge success and even my photographs are all right. One of the pilots asks me if I was at all frightened and when I say I was quite OK, except just before we pulled out of the dive, this produces much merriment. In fact, after this it is part of every pilot's job to take me up on test flights in order to try and scare me a little. This exercise is known as "frightening the doc"!

For two or three weeks the atmosphere on the station is quite holiday-like, and I go up with someone or other two or three times a week.

This pleasant arrangement does have its unsafe moments, however. There is the time when a new, rather carefree, pilot joins the squadron—and as usual asks if I would like to come up on a test flight. About a mile off Malta, at about 4000 feet, he asks "Have you ever been in a spin?" I say "No" and he says "Well, I'll show you one" and he promptly eases the throttle back and suddenly the aeroplane goes into a spin. Now, in the back seat the centrifugal force is more than in the pilot's seat and, as the aircraft spins faster and faster, I gradually become rather giddy and muzzy. The sea is approaching at an alarming speed, when suddenly we go into a very violent manoeuvre just above the water, which involves putting the nose right down.

I really think my last moment has come, but with a violent jerk we come out of the spin about 30 feet above the sea. There is silence from my pilot, then over the intercom comes "Are you all right doc?" I say I am, then surprisingly, "Were you frightened?" I said I was. Then from the pilot comes "So was I—I forgot we had a torpedo on board and I couldn't get her out of the spin". We fly rather sedately back to Malta, with a rather subdued pilot and by mutual agreement decide not to say anything about the episode. I reckon this is the nearest I have ever been to sudden death.

Strangely enough we become good friends after this and I remember him with real affection. He was so young and carefree and gay. Later, events were to produce a sort of instant maturity in him, which was rather sad.

All this, of course, means that I get to know the aircrews very well as I am living with them now in the mess, up on the station.

The CO is a young man with a cherubic face and quite bald on top. He is a regular RN lieutenant commander, and his pilot also is a regular RN lieutenant (two stripes). They have absolute confidence in each other and are totally unflappable; they are the backbone and basis of the high morale of the squadron. The rest of them are RNVR pilots and observers, all hastily trained during the first years of the war. Most of them are aged about 20 or so—with just a sprinkling of older ones.

Each pilot sticks to his own observer and they are nearly

always to be seen in pairs whatever they are doing at all times, day or night. The observers are always very busy, because they are in charge of a new top secret gadget (a mobile radar) which they carry in the rear cockpit. This is supposed to "home them in" on shipping targets at night and they have to cope with this, as well as the navigation.

Just before I arrive on the scene the squadron has suffered a lot of losses and we have had four or five replacement pairs.

After about a fortnight the holiday-like atmosphere gradually evaporates as night operations against enemy convoys are gradually stepped up. Everything becomes rather grim again and no one has time for play or jokes any more.

Nearly every night one or two crews go out either singly or together to patrol at maximum range, trying to find supply ships or convoys, with their new radar gadget. I usually see them off from the control tower, grab a few hours sleep, then get back to the control tower to welcome them back and have a very early "operational breakfast" with them, which they seem to appreciate.

One week, two crews just disappear. They fail to come back and are lost without trace. This casts a great gloom over everybody. On two occasions there is hair-raising worry as pilots approaching home report themselves so short of petrol that they don't think they will make it.

In each case they do *just* make it with only a dribble in the tank, and two very shaken young men climb out of the plane.

Once a pair come back with the story that they had hit and sunk an ammunition ship, which had exploded and gone down in flames. It is the same young pilot who had nearly killed me in a spin! Everybody congratulates him and his observer, but I can see that this experience has shaken him to the core. The usual smile is wiped off his face and he is no longer his usual cheery self.

This sort of thing cannot go on for very long without some effect on the pilots—and the effect is not very long coming. One pilot and observer pair after a near squeak in returning to Malta one night, show a sudden change in behaviour. They become silent and morose and start drinking more than is good for them. They are young, recently trained and it is all too clear that the whole thing has become too much for them. They have got "the twitch" which is pilot slang for sudden loss of self-confidence. There is a strange premonition of disaster which hangs over them.

Two or three nights later they go out on a nocturnal routine torpedo mission and they just disappear! They are never heard of again. Gloom among the pilots deepens, but worse is to come.

The CO, the experienced, quiet, unflappable lieutenant commander, who is the real backbone of the squadron is suddenly posted home—*without his pilot*. His pilot, who has flown with him all the time and looks like a thoroughly dependable, well trained, RN lieutenant, is suddenly given command of the squadron. What happens?

I cannot believe it, but before my eyes this rock-like young man goes to pieces. He becomes silent and morose, drinks (which he never did before) and chooses a new observer in whom he obviously has no confidence. The sign of death is upon him. Sure enough on the very next mission his Albacore simply disappears.

It is awful—even more awful because the Eighth Army is now in Tripoli and the battle of the Mediterranean and North Africa is practically over. The loss of both these crews was really quite unnecessary. And I firmly believe that these young men *knew* that they were doomed, that they had a premonition of death.

After these two losses most of the night operations cease as the great battle of North Africa comes to its triumphant conclusion. The squadron relaxes, slowly the pilots are posted to other squadrons, and a feeling of change comes over the airfield.

The invasion of Sicily is in the air and suddenly a whole Spitfire wing comes to Hal Far. All is turmoil and excitement.

Our quiet and well-ordered mess is suddenly full of bubbling young Spitfire pilots. In the evening there is a great concourse round the bar and the gin flows freely. A new wing commander, flying, has appeared. He is a tall fair-haired, very extrovert individual known as Cocky Dundas and he chats up everyone at the bar. The new arrivals are all very elated and seem to be looking forward to the next phase of the war. All this is very different from the grim atmosphere on the island when I first arrived. Excitement comes to me too, as I am suddenly posted to Gozo. But that is another story.

〰〰〰〰〰〰〰〰

FIGURE 1. The author (on left), and one of the pilots of 185 Squadron standing outside our very bombed and strafed 'sick quarters' at RAF Hal Far in October 1942. Note the bomb and cannon shell scars on the stone-work!

FIGURE 2. The author, standing in exactly the same place (at sick quarters Hal Far), but 45 years later in 1987. The building had been patched up and was now being used as a school for the disabled.

FIGURE 3. A DC 3 coming in to land (on one engine).

FIGURE 4. A DC 3 loading casualties at a desert airfield. Note the steel mesh laid down over the sand, which constitutes the temporary runway.

FIGURE 5. Spitfire pilots of 185 Squadron lined up outside their much bombed mess building at Hal Far in 1942. Third from the right, in battle dress is Wing Cdr Prosser-Hanks DSO DFC, (station commander) and on his right is Sqdr. Leader White (CO of 185 Squadron).

FIGURE 6. These are the "erks", who lived round the Spitfire pens, serviced the Spitfires and generally kept them flying. They were indiscriminately bombed, ordered about and expected to be on hand at any hour of the day or night. They are the unsung heroes of the siege of Malta.

FIGURE 7. An Albacore (with torpedo) standing near a Spitfire anti-blast pen, at Hal Far airfield in 1943.

FIGURE 8. Torpedo-carrying albacores in flight.

FIGURE 9. Pilots and observers of 827 and 828 Squadrons of the Fleet Air Arm, on Malta in 1943, lined up against the wing of one of their Albacores.

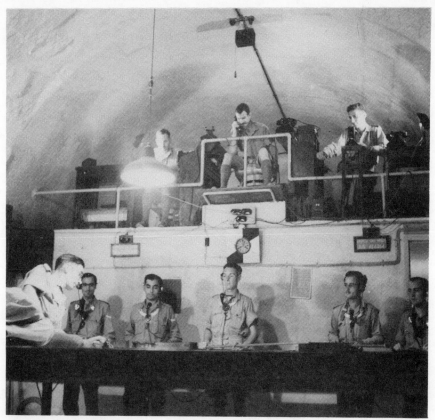

FIGURE 10. The Malta fighter operations room in session.

FIGURE 11. The author looking out over the old Hal Far airfield from the original old control tower in 1987. A derelict DC3 is in the background.

FIGURE 12. A derelict DC3 on Hal Far airfield in 1987. It is now being used for fire-fighting instruction.

FIGURE 13. Standing on the western end of the old run-way at Xewkija, Gòzo in 1987. The large "cathedral" was not there in 1943. The local Gozitan to whom we are speaking was a boy of 12 at the time of the Gozo airfield in 1943 and remembered it perfectly.

FIGURE 14. Standing on the eastern end of the old run-way at Xewkija, Gozo in 1987. A few old oil drums can be seen, but otherwise no trace of it. It was now "a quiet field of onions, tomatoes and cabbages".

FIGURE 15. Xlendi Bay, Gozo. This lovely, formerly deserted, inlet is now a favourite spot for visitors. In 1943 only the four little buildings on the right were there. One of them, St Patrick's Hotel, is still there and still functioning as a tiny hotel.

CHAPTER 5

GONE TO GOZO

".. . the horse-flies spear my tender legs with great zest, *through* my
socks . . ."

FIVE

GONE TO GOZO

It is mid June 1943 and I have just landed at the little port of Mgarr in Gozo. It is very hot, and I'm dressed in tropical kit namely, jacket, shorts and long socks up to my knees. The first thing that happens is that a horde of large horse-flies settle on me and start attacking. I've never met animals like this, it's like having lots of injections at the same time with a blunt needle. They particularly like my socks (I suppose the texture is like a donkey's fur!) and they spear my tender legs with great zest, *through* my socks.

I hop about, and only some very athletic and continuous antics keep them at bay. I'm really glad when a beaten-up old 15 cwt Dodge van comes in sight. This is the RAF transport, and I climb aboard in a great hurry to get away from this accursed spot.

How did I come to be chosen as "Medical Officer— Gozo", a very small and practically unnoticed part of the great plan for "Operation Husky"—the invasion of Sicily?

The whole thing is a wonderful illustration of the old saying "from small beginnings great events do spring".

As I've already explained there are two medical officers on Hal Far airfield. I am the junior. The senior one hogs what actual medical work there is and I get very bored, as I don't seem to have anything to do. I hang around sick quarters and get under the skin of my medical colleagues. One day, while complaining about this he says, "for God's sake shut up and find something to do—why don't you go and inspect all the billets where the airmen live"?

At first this sounded most dreary and unexciting, but on second thoughts it had one or two definite attractions. These were, (1) it would get me off the station for a bit as most of the airmen were billeted in the neighbouring village of Birzebuggia, and (2) it would give me a cast iron excuse to use one of the station jeeps.

So off I go to the adjutant to get a list of the billets, then to the transport section to beg for a jeep and I have something to do for at least a week.

Well, this business rapidly proves a real eye-opener for me because the men are housed in the most awful circumstances you could wish to see. Most of them are crammed into tiny airless rooms in the back of small Maltese houses in the village. They have no beds—only straw palliases, which are mostly verminous. Washing and toilet facilities are practically non-existent. There is one blanket per man. They eat their rations wherever they can find somewhere to sit down, mostly round the aircraft dispersal pens on the airfield.

How they manage to remain as healthy as they are is a miracle.

They have simply been dumped hurriedly in these damaged houses when the battle of Malta was at its height and nobody has taken any further notice of them—as long as they turn up and do their duty. They are a most uncomplaining lot, and as my inspection goes on, my heart is touched and I get really involved. Most of the billets have large black bed-bugs climbing out of the walls, with which the airmen fight a continuous but losing battle. These animals are really malignant. They come out at night and bite the sleeping airmen when they are nice and warm. The bites, which are mostly on the arms and legs, then turn into painful infected ulcers—which I have been treating up at my sick quarters without really knowing the cause until now. I would say about 20% of the airman are affected—some quite badly.

They welcome me as I am the first person to take any interest in their living conditions.

I go back to the station and write a stinking report on all this. One copy goes to the commanding officer and another to the principal medical officer in Valletta.

Well, it couldn't have caused more of a stir if I'd dropped a bomb on the place.

First, I'm hauled up before the station commanding officer, who has actually read my report and seems to approve of my activities. I am sent off with the adjutant to find new and better billets for the men; we spend several pleasant afternoons in the jeep exploring Birzebuggia and its environs and gradually re-house the men.

Next, if you please, we get a visit from the high and mighty—namely, the PMO (Principal Medical Officer)—who has the awe-inspiring rank of group captain. He is a pleasant, brisk character with a little toothbrush moustache. He comes into our bombed out sick quarters, inspects them and chats to everyone affably. Then he comes in and has a mug of coffee with us (the two doctors). He has obviously read my great report and is interested in what we are doing about it—and wants to see a ruined tennis court that I resurrected in my spare time on the station. He seems to know quite a lot about me; he knows that I did a resident surgical job for a year before I joined up and he asks me a bit about my surgical experience.

It gradually dawns on me that I am suddenly something of a "blue-eyed boy" at medical headquarters in Valetta. An unusual experience for me!

I was not to know that a very interesting job is just coming up and that I am being considered for it.

Soon after all this we get another visit by the PMO but this time he takes me aside and says, would I like to go to Gozo and provide medical cover for the forces there during the invasion of Sicily?

Would I! I certainly would, it sounds marvellous. I'd be on my own with complete responsibility for all service personnel in Gozo. There might be some proper medical work to do and, who knows, maybe even some surgery.

When does he want me to go? Straight away—tomorrow.

So, I pack a small bag and my "officer's camp kit", report

to Valetta medical headquarters for a few (very few) instructions and I'm on my way to the end of the island, where a small boat picks me up and ferries me over to the port of Mgarr in Gozo.

That's how I come to be standing on the smelly old quay being attacked by this pack of horseflies on a sunny afternoon this June in the year of our Lord 1943.

CHAPTER 6

Gozo 1

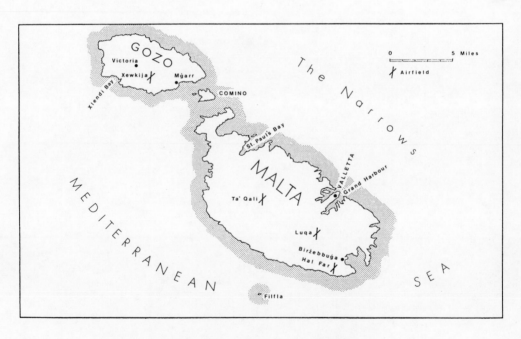

Map showing location of main airfields.

SIX

Gozo 1

G ozo looks a quiet and sleepy little island. That is my first impression, as we bump along the dirt road towards the centre of the island. Suddenly, we come in sight of a lot of tents of a dark green khaki colour. This is the American camp, tucked away at the foot of a small hill. Here I am met by a young RAF flying officer, who is acting adjucant. He takes me into a tent with a few trestle tables and benches, which is the mess where everyone feeds. There is an American field kitchen here in full operation. You line up with your individual mess tin and mug and a hot mess of potatoes, meat and vegetables, plus some sort of stewed fruit is sloshed into it—all mixed up together! It is hot and, as we are very hungry, it tastes delicious.

The Americans are from an engineer battalion who have been on the island for about a fortnight making the airfield. They come from Tunis and, apparently, the airstrip is nearly finished already.

Next I make contact with the other half of "the medical cover for this island". This consists of an inoffensive young medical orderly and a driver. I discover that the beaten-up old Dodge 15 cwt truck that brought me up from the harbour is, in fact, my ambulance and general transport. It has two tents in it and a couple of wooden chests with a red cross on them containing medical supplies. I get in and we set off in search of the airfield.

Gozo is a hilly, uneven little island, and we suddenly come upon the airstrip round a bend in the narrow lane we are on. It really is very impressive, even more so when one realizes that it has been constructed in a fortnight flat.

The American engineers simply chose one of the few relatively flat areas, lined up their bulldozers and an airstrip came out behind them! This is no mean feat as the island is irregular, rocky and criss-crossed by lots of stone walls which divide up the small fields and stop the earth being blown away. It is a full-scale fighter airfield and the dirt runways are covered with the fine steel mesh which has been used so successfully on temporary airstrips in the desert campaign. Many of the locals are putting the finishing touches to some stone-walled "pens" which will house the fighter planes when they arrive.

Now, the urgent problem is where to set up my "medical centre". I find a likely-looking field just by the runway but at a lower level. It has an access road (or rather track) and a sort of ramp going up on to the runway proper—so that my truck can drive up on to the side of the runway and be on hand for any crashes. It seems a good spot, so we pitch our two tents, a small one for me and a bigger one, which is the medical tent proper. The medical orderly sleeps in the bigger tent on a stretcher. We also have a flag pole with a Red Cross flag which we put up. I feel we are really in business now!

Well, we work away the whole afternoon and about 6 pm five or six rather lost looking RAF chaps appear. I thought maybe they were patients, but no such luck. They turn out to be an RAF regiment unit who have been setting up an AA battery for defence of the airfield. Their officer has disappeared somewhere and their problem is that they are hungry and they have no rations and, in fact, appear singularly helpless.

Now in my week's training course in England after joining up, they taught me what was expected of an RAF officer. One of the duties of a good officer, apparently, is "to see that the troops are fed *before* attending to one's own requirement". Right, I think, now is the time to show a few officer-like qualities. So, I bundle them all into my Dodge truck and off we all go to the American mess. There, I explain the problem and these splendid Yanks give them all a mess tin and line them up in front of the cooks and there is general bliss. I meet the young adjutant again and we hang around until the troops are fed. Then, in an excess of officer-like quality, we put the now beaming and grateful troops back in my truck and run them back to the airfield and their sleeping tents by the AA gun.

We, the adjutant and I, both feel very responsible and self-satisfied after this display of initiative and we also notice that we, ourselves, are very hungry. In fact, ravenously hungry.

So, back we go to the American mess. Horror of horrors! The cooks' tents are empty and the rations have been locked away. They have "closed shop" for the day! We cannot scrounge anything at all.

By now, we are both painfully hungry so we climb in the truck and go back to the airfield, to my tent.

We go for a stroll in the fields near the airstrip with some vague hope of finding something.

We do find something. We find a small tent with a man sitting in front of it, fingering a rifle. We approach him rather gingerly as he looks anything but promising.

He is dirty, unshaven and looks like a pirate or criminal of some sort. He is dressed in a torn, greasy old battle jacket and khaki tropical trousers—but, on his shoulder scarcely visible for dirt are the two stripes of an RAF flight lieutenant!

It turns out that he is the officer in charge of the RAF regiment detachment, with the AA gun on the airfield. He is a very surly character indeed, and we rather timidly put our problem to him about not having had anything to eat all day. At this he eyes us with great scorn. He says he is just about to eat himself and disappears into the tent.

He comes out with a small battered tin of corned beef. We are somewhat disappointed and ask him if that is all he has got. "No" he says, "that's not all I've got, and if you had the sense to look, you would see that there is food all around you". We look rather non-plussed at this and must have shown it, for he then says "You're standing in the middle of a field of onions, you fools".

He gives us an old bayonet and tells us to dig up some onions, peel them and slice them. Having done this we return and find an old primus stove in action, with slices of corned beef frying in a mess tin.

We pour our peeled onions in to it and in no time at all the night air is filled with the delicious aroma of steak and onions.

We sit on the ground and partake of this feast, washed down by a somewhat suspect bottle of wine. Our host does not talk much and, obviously, has a very low opinion of us. Apparently, he has been right through the desert campaign and is used to fending for himself in all circumstances, unlike us who he regards as a pair of useless ninnies.

We are not allowed inside the tent, though I can just catch a glimpse of quite a lot of interesting bottles and tins. Our host, I think, is the original entrepreneur and, I suspect, has spent the day flogging RAF rations to the locals and certainly not looking after the welfare of his men! In spite of his surly attitude towards us we end the evening well fed and happy and I turn in, in my camp bed in my tent, without a care in the world.

Next morning, up early, a shave and a splash in my canvas camp wash basin and thoughts on the new day. This is the life, I think. Sick parade is at 9 am, I have put up a notice to this effect. However, no patients!

Now, I give this matter of being in medical charge of the island during the Sicily invasion some thought. What I need is, a hospital.

I put on my clean tropical uniform (shorts, bush jacket and suede boots) and drive off to the capital of Gozo—a small medieval town called Victoria, dominated by a large castle and cathedral. Here, in the middle of the little town, in a delightful square, I find the old hospital.

It is a lovely old building, made of stone, like everything else on the island, which has weathered to a mature light grey. Inside, there is a quiet courtyard flanked by two long wards. The whole thing is run by nuns in long white habits. I find the mother superior who sends for an English nun, who turns out to be quite young and pleasant looking. She is the interpreter as the mother superior speaks no English. I wonder how the young nun came to be here?

I explain my problem, that for a short time there are going to be a lot of air force people on the island and there might be some casualties. She is fairly co-operative, but for some reason averts her eyes from me whilst talking. They take me off to see the operating theatre which is small and sparsely furnished, though adequate. The sister in charge proudly shows me an array of gleaming instruments—mostly very antique and obviously, almost never used. Being a budding surgeon I really fall for this small theatre and hospital. I hope I shall have something to do here.

What luck—I have a hospital, theatre, beds and, willing nurses all on my doorstep.

As I go to leave the young English nun appears, very troubled and confused, and wishes to speak to me privately. She asks me if I could possibly wear long trousers when I visit the hospital, as the sight of my bare knees upsets the nuns. This was the reason why the mother superior averted her eyes whilst talking to me!

Apparently, this particular order is not supposed to look upon bare male flesh (except the face, presumably!) I am suitably apologetic and I promise to wear long trousers.

The airfield is practically complete. Air Vice Marshall Park (AOC Malta) has flown over to look at it, and we are to expect a whole fighter wing in the next couple of days with all their attendant ground crews, controllers and so on. This means that up to two or three hundred men will be descending on this sleepy little island and mostly living under canvas.

I retire to my tent and consider the matter with the help of the *Medical officers' field service manual*. What should I be doing? The book says, that the water supply of any new site must be checked carefully and if, in any doubt, chlorine tablets must be added to sterilize the water. The concentration of chlorine must be about 0.04 per cent and I have even got a kit to estimate this concentration.

So, off I go to the town hall in Victoria to the public health department (one small room with desk and two chairs). I present my credentials saying that I am in charge of the health of all the troops coming on to the island and I would like to inspect the water supply. I am given a minor official—a Gozitan who speaks very poor English, and we set off in my truck.

The next hour or so truly astounds me. The water supply of Gozo must be one of the natural wonders of the world. I am taken underground into a series of enormous natural caves or grottos, hollowed out of the solid rock. Fresh water seeps out of the rock continuously and is channelled by hundreds of small rivulets into one central river, which leads to the central reservoir, which is a sort of underground lake. The whole set-up is incredibly ancient and has been supplying the lucky Gozitans with pure fresh water for centuries.

I am quite lost in admiration at this wonder of nature. But, aha! What have we here! Just where the main river enters the pipe to the reservoir there is a little apparatus which gives about one drip per minute of a white cloudy liquid into the flowing water. It is a primitive chlorination apparatus! How much chlorine is in the water, I ask? To my astonishment my small Gozitan companion knows the figure—it is 0.01 per cent, he says.

Well, my book says to be safe it should be 0.04 per cent. So, assuming an air of authority and wisdom, I say this is not safe enough for our troops and I must increase the concentration. By a simple calculation this entails increasing the drip rate, from one per minute to four per minute. I do this by carefully turning the old glass stopcock until we have reached the appropriate rate.

My companion is horrified at this action and is very worried by what I have done. But, I am adamant that we must have a higher chlorine concentration, and we leave.

I feel rather pleased with myself over this. I've probably prevented a typhoid epidemic amongst the troops by this simple bit of preventative medicine, I think.

However, the sequel comes about two days later when two gentlemen appear at my medical tent intent on seeing me urgently. Hoping that this might be some medical emergency I see them at once. One of them is my small Gozitan official and the other is a well dressed and well spoken Maltese gentleman. He, it turns out, is in charge of the public water supply in Malta and loses no time in telling me how concerned he is about my stepping up the chlorination of Gozo's water supply. Apparently, anything higher than 0.01 per cent chlorine is liable to eat away and crack the ancient channels and stone pipes in the underground water galleries of Gozo.

I show him my book but this only seems to make him angry and he more or less tells me that he is not having the whole water supply system of Gozo ruined, just because a few troops are on the island. He, quite rightly, points out that the risk of typhoid and other disease is worse with cracked pipes! I am forced to accede to his greater experience and he marches off to slow the chlorine drip down to one drop per minute again.

That is really the end of my public health effort on Gozo and I decide I shall concentrate on surgery from now on!

CHAPTER 7

Gozo 2

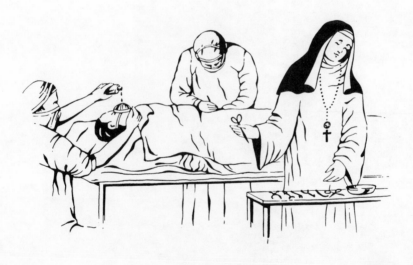

". . . why is sister looking away, and why won't she come into the
operating theatre?"

SEVEN

Gozo 2

I t is now the 23rd day of June and excitement grips us as the
aeroplanes of the fighter wing sweep in to land in quick
succession. It turns out to be an American fighter wing flying
reverse-lend-lease Spitfires, and very expert they are. The
Spitfires have American markings, which seems very odd!

The transformation of Gozo is utter and complete, from a
sleepy little island into a hive of bustle and activity. Aeroplanes
landing, ground crews hustling them off to the dispersal pens,
tents springing up everywhere, suddenly and mysteriously there
are lots of people—all very busy.

I spend a lot of my time now in my Dodge truck at the side
of the airfield, watching the flying, and trying to glean scraps of
information about what's going on, from anybody willing to talk.
They are all very discreet and nobody lets on about the date of the
invasion of Sicily. In fact, most of them are as much in the dark as
I am. It's a well kept secret.

Suddenly a small convoy of three jeeps turns off the road
and draws up outside my medical tent. An American major gets
out, who introduces himself as the senior medical officer of the
American wing. He says "hullo", walks around, sniffs round a bit,
and says "Well, I guess this is as good as anywhere, do you mind if
we settle in alongside you?" I say, no, in fact I am delighted. His

boys get busy, and in no time at all there is what looks like a small field hospital alongside my two little tents. There are about five medical GIs, and the whole set up is highly professional. It rather dwarfs my little effort.

However, the major is a quite delightful person and we are soon fast friends. His name is White, and he turns out to be the doctor who went with the Doolittle raid over Tokyo (the first American bomber raid of the war). The bombers took off from an aircraft carrier, as near as they could get to Japan, bombed Tokyo, and then flew straight on into the depths of China, where they landed at a remote airfield. Most of them then managed to make their way overland back to civilization.

Apart from this he has quite extensive experience of traumatic surgery. He regales me with stories of when he was an intern in a New York hospital, where knife fights and bullet wounds were commonplace, every night affairs! All this has obviously fitted him for war surgery very well. My own life and experience seems terribly humdrum after all this, but I am bound to say he is a wonderfully stimulating companion. Moreover we can now work a roster, whereby one of us is always on duty on the airfield, when the other is away.

I spend most of the rest of the day with him being shown the tented American officers' mess, and meeting a few of the pilots. Once again the Americans feed me very well.

The following morning, his medical tent is very busy. He seems to have loads of patients, while I only have about three!

But one of my three patients has a bad abdominal pain, and has typical acute appendicitis! Now this is really my cup of tea! I really do know how to deal with this.

I get the patient into the back of my Dodge truck and off we go to the little hospital in Victoria, and he is soon in bed, the only patient! I then inform the mother superior that I propose to operate for acute appendicitis at three o'clock. This throws the whole hospital into a state of turmoil. The mother superior calls for the theatre sister, who is quietly excited by it all and gives me a conducted tour round the instruments available. These, in fact, are very good—quite adequate for the occasion. But there is one big snag—where do we find an anaesthetist? There is apparently a visiting doctor, who still lives on the island, and a messenger is sent to fetch him. He turns out to be a pleasant young Maltese called Tabone, with slicked back black hair, and large horn rimmed glasses. Yes, he had been taught how to give open ether anaesthesia at his medical school, and had actually given one or two anaesthetics several years ago in Malta. In spite of this lack of recent experience he is prepared to "have a go" for me. We check in the hospital dispensary and there are indeed several bottles of ether there. So, we are all set!

At three o'clock the patient is wheeled into the tiny, but spotless operating theatre, and young Dr Tabone starts dripping ether onto the open lint mask over his face.

The patient, who has been well premedicated, reacts very well and is soon asleep and breathing regularly and deeply. Meanwhile I have stripped the patient, shaved the appropriate area, and painted the skin with iodine solution. I then wash up and don gown and gloves, and then re-enter the little theatre to begin the operation.

Where is sister and her tray of instruments? She is next door, in the next room and she won't come into the theatre! What is wrong? The English speaking sister is summoned, and she explains that sister can't come into the theatre until the patient is properly covered up. Its this old problem of bare male flesh again—like my knees!

So I take the sterile towels off her trolley and trot into the theatre and drape the patient so that there is only one tiny square of iodine covered flesh showing, on the right hand side of the abdomen, where I am going to operate. Sister then re-appears, all is well, and we get on with the operation. Sister is very good once she gets going, Dr Tabone steadily drips ether at the other end, and I remove a very nasty gangrenous appendix.

As often happens in these far from ideal conditions, the patient makes an absolutely normal recovery, without any complications whatever! Everybody at the little hospital is very bucked, and pleased at their contribution to the war effort. Dr Tabone is so pleased with himself and his prowess as anaesthetist that he is looking for another patient. He also asks me how it is that I can diagnose appendicitis so confidently, which rather shakes me, as he has obviously never seen a case before.

However, all in all, medical morale is now at a high. Even Major White is slightly impressed when I recount the day's doings, later on over a friendly drink in his tent.

The next few days are fairly routine, there is a lot of flying, and I am on the strip most of the time.

I usually hold a sick parade at nine o'clock, for seldom more than three or four patients. The Americans have a much bigger practice—but, of course, there are quite a lot of them on the island now.

VIPs fly in and inspect the place and fly off again—I get a brief glimpse of personalities like Air Vice Marshal Keith Park. Also our friendly PMO (principal medical officer) flies in for a visit and seems satisfied with what he sees. He is much amused and impressed by the appendicitis episode. He doesn't think much of the site of my medical tent, however, which is about half way down the runway. He thinks it ought to be nearer "headquarters".

I refrain from telling him that I haven't the foggiest notion where headquarters are (even if they exist). They are probably in one of the tents or possibly in one of the mysterious caravans which are parked and camouflaged near the end of the runway.

In fact one of the extraordinary things about the whole set-up is the way it seems to run itself without any visible higher direction. Everybody just gets on with the war in their own sweet way.

One night, a few days later I am awakened by a great deal of activity in the American tent next door, round about 2 am. There is so much coming and going that I get up and go over to see if they need any help. "No thank you", they say, "we're OK."

So I go back, but there is no more sleep for me that night. There is continuous coming and going, loud talking, and occasional laughter from next door, right up to about 5 am. I am mystified!

After sick parade next morning I step over to Major White, and ask him what on earth was going on last night? He is a little shame-faced about the explanation.

Apparently a certain Gozitan lady had a rather simple, but strapping daughter. She became aware that hundreds of sex-hungry American GIs were on the island—roaming around for "satisfaction". After one or two GIs had "propositioned" her with regard to her daughter, and offered her dollars, she suddenly became aware that there were considerable financial possibilities in the affair. Accordingly she let the aforesaid GIs know that she would be in business that evening. The word spread like wildfire among the GIs, and instead of two or three, there was a queue of 20 or more by midnight. This, of course, represents a small fortune for a Gozitan peasant and so they both set to with a will all night on an opportunity which obviously might never occur again.

Now all American GIs are taught that after intercourse with the local girls, it is necessary to have what they call a "pro". This is short for prophylactic and consists of coming at once to the medical orderly and having a bit of mercury ointment squeezed up the urethra, and a good wash of the genital region in a strong antiseptic. This performance is supposed to keep them free of any venereal disease. It probably does work. This is what they were doing in the American medical tent, all night long, for an apparently endless stream of GIs!

Fortunately (or unfortunately depending on one's point of view) this promising little business is promptly closed down by the American CO after Major White reports on the nights doings!

At least it means the rest of us get a decent night's sleep again!

~~~~~~~~~~~~~~~~~~

CHAPTER 8

Gozo 3

". . . it's an American Tomahawk fighter . . . he comes in fast and low
pursued by my ambulance . . ."

EIGHT

Gozo 3

Well, things seem to be hotting up on the strip quite a bit. There is greatly increased activity with the Spitfire squadron who seem to be taking off and landing several times a day, which means I spend a lot of time on the strip. There are no casualties, all the pilots are very competent, but they kick up a lot of dust on and around the dried up runway. Everybody and everything is covered in a light brown layer of it, including the inside of my medical tent.

It's 10 July and judging by the air activity the invasion of Sicily must be going on about now, but we are dreadfully cut off on Gozo and nobody tells us exactly what is occurring.

During the afternoon there is the first emergency on the strip. I am told that there is a plane about to make an emergency landing, with damage to its brakes and flaps. OK, I am ready. I get in the ambulance and rev up the engine, with the fire tender beside me. The plane in question turns out to be an American Tomahawk fighter, not based at Gozo, with the huge grinning sharks' teeth painted on the forward part of the fuselage. He comes in low and lands on the end of the strip but, much too fast, and as he approaches the end of the runway it is obvious that he cannot stop himself. However, just before he hits the end of the runway, he applies full left rudder suddenly and the aircraft gently keels over on its right wing and slithers to a halt, in a cloud of dust.

I am overcome with admiration at this clever manoeuvre and I race my ambulance up the plane, jump out and on to the wing, just as the pilot is undoing his safety harness. He is a tough grizzled looking American and, obviously, in a very bad temper.

He is very surprised at suddenly seeing a strange young chap on his wing, just as he is about to get out quickly. I say to him, "Are you alright"? He replies, "Who the hell are you? Get off my wing". I haven't even time to explain that I am the doctor before he walks away in a great huff. I can't say I blame him. However, I do have the satisfaction of being right on the spot if anything nasty had happened!

The other bit of excitement occurs just before dusk. Before turning in, I am taking a quiet stroll by the edge of the strip when, to my amazement, I see a fairly large aircraft making for the strip in absolute silence. Suddenly, I realize it's a glider and it seems to be making for the patch of land just to the right of the strip. I jump into the American jeep, which happens to be standing just there, and drive off in haste towards its obvious landing area. It comes down and glides very roughly and jerkily to a sudden jolting halt, and I am on the spot at once.

It doesn't seem to be an enemy glider but, in fact, I can't see any markings in the dusk. So, perhaps rather foolishly, I dash up to the door of the glider and to my surprise it opens quite easily. I put my head inside and it is full of troops. They all seem unnaturally still, as if they were stunned, so I say "Hello, everybody". I wonder what on earth is wrong and then, suddenly, it hits me. The stench of concentrated vomit and sickness in that small crowded glider is unbelievable. I reel back to take a gulp of fresh air.

The pilot, who is draped over his seat, appears almost unconscious and says, "Where are we"?

I reply, "Gozo".

He says, "Where is that? Are we behind the lines?"

"No", I say, "You're in Gozo, which is just near Malta and you are just near an RAF air-strip".

At this, there is a noticeable stirring amongst the prostrate bodies in the glider: something like a sigh of relief. But, everybody in that aircraft is absolutely and totally prostrate, with air-sickness. The first thing to do is somehow to get them out of that awful stench, so I help first the pilot and then several men to get out, and lay them on the ground. Of course, within a minute the fresh air, and the even more reassuring knowledge that they are among friends, and don't have to start fighting an ememy, has a marvellous effect and they sit up and go and haul out the rest of the troops who are still totally disabled inside. The fresh air works it's miracle and within about five minutes, they are all sitting up, relaxing, and congratulating themselves on being alive, tremendously relieved at not having to fight. They are all English glider-borne troops.

At this point, I realize that I must have been the only person to notice the glider's descent, so I leave them and buzz off in my jeep to tell somebody about it. I find some people at the end of the runway and tell them that a lot of airborne troops have just landed. After a brief period of disbelief, they get hold of two more jeeps and some American officers come to investigate.

By the time we all get back to the glider the troops have all recovered and are sitting around talking and laughing gaily. In fact, there is a distinct picnic-like quality about the whole affair.

Apparently, they had been towed by an American plane, with the intention of coming down behind the German lines in Sicily somewhere. However, the plane had lost its way completely and was running short of fuel when, suddenly, they saw land beneath them. The glider had been cast free without more ado and they came down, grateful to be on dry land, but without the foggiest notion where they were. The glider had had an extremely rough ride and, gradually, the whole lot of them became totally prostrated with air sickness.

I cannot help feeling that it is just as well that they landed on friendly territory, as I could have taken the whole lot prisoner, single handed, when I opened the door of that glider as no one was capable of even moving, let alone putting up any resistance!

Well, all's well that ends well. The now joyful and relieved troops are all carted off in the jeeps and bedded down in tents.

Well, the next three days or so are full of activity. One day two DC 3 transport planes land. One of them is full of American casualties and out of the other steps Air Vice Marshal Harry Broadhust, who is AOC Desert Air Force and a very big shot indeed.

I go round the casualties with Major White and we sort out the worst ones, who are transferred to Broadhurst's DC 3 as, he is going near one of the base hospitals in North Africa. The casualties are very cheerful. They nearly all have drips up, mostly to combat dehydration. They have all been expertly treated and there is little for me to do, other than help get them into the right aeroplane.

I even have a brief conversation with Harry Broadhust himself, who seems quite pleased to see me. So, for a brief moment, I feel almost at the centre of things and actually involved in the invasion! This appears to be going well according to the chat I pick up from various members of the Broadhurst entourage.

Next morning, in the middle of all this, on my sick parade, there is *another* British airman with acute appendicitis. I can't really believe it, there can't be more than 100 or so RAF types on the island (mostly RAF Regiment) and it is unbelievable that they should produce *two* cases of acute appendicitis.

This time my team goes into action very smoothly. I take the patient into my little hospital in Victoria, issue instructions and, later on that afternoon, Gozo's second appendicectomy takes place. Dr Tabone gives the anaesthetic, as to the manner born, sister takes to me like an old hand and the diagnosis again proves correct, as another nasty inflamed appendix is removed.

The tiny hospital and the nuns all take me for granted now and the whole atmosphere is much easier, with coffee and cakes in sister's room after the operation, just like an ordinary operating session in England. I wear long trousers and the nuns come and go as they please and several of them actually talk to me. I am really intrigued by the young English nun who looks very pleasant. I wonder how she came to be here, in the middle of a war? It is quite certain, however, that I'm not going to find out, even though they are all much mor relaxed.

After about three days or so things seem much quieter.

That evening, I have a great farewell dinner down at Xlendi Bay with Major White, the American medical officer. He tells that, tomorrow, he is leaving the island as his fighter wing is moving to Sicily! We drink a little too much and sing some noisy songs.

~~~~~~~~~~~~~~~~~~~~~~~

CHAPTER 9

GOZO – DECLINE

FERTILIS AB UNDIS
CAPUT EFFERO

Gozo's (unofficial but generally used and accepted) **Coat-of-Arms** is a stylized representation of what a visitor's first glimpse is like: three hills (usually taken to be Zebbug, Xaghra and Nadur) in green (to show the island's agricultural fertility) on a blue sea. The (optional) star refers both to peace and to the nice weather. The motto can be freely translated as 'I raise a fertile head from the sea'.

NINE

GOZO – DECLINE

The invasion has passed over us and the Spitfires and their pilots and ground crews have all gone to airfields in Sicily. It is very hot and everything is quiet again.

Here I am with my little tented sick quarters and absolutely nothing to do again!

The American camp has moved on and so there is nowhere to eat! As the airfield is quite dead, with practically no activity, I move my sleeping quarters to a room near St Patrick's Hotel, in Xlendi Bay, about two miles away on the coast.

Xlendi is a small but deep inlet, in the rocky coast. Along the tiny quay there are about five stone houses. My room, on the first floor, is in one of these facing the sea. I have breakfast and the evening meal at the small hotel. There are some brightly coloured fishing boats in the harbour and so there is plenty of fish, which is what I have most nights.

In other circumstances, it would be an idyllic existence but there is no one to talk to and I feel forgotten.

Today, even the RAF Regiment contingent leaves the island but, before they go, they make the airstrip unserviceable by putting large oil drums, filled with stones, all over it. This is so that enemy planes can't land here! Then they leave the island! As far as I can see, I'm the only one left and I feel very ill. I still have my Dodge 15 cwt truck, so I take it down to Xlendi and go to bed. In the morning I feel awful, I've got a temperature of 102 degrees.

I can't do anything except drink water all day and try vainly to keep cool. I have a frightful headache too.

Next day is the same. I take loads of aspirin and manage to consult my tropical diseases handbook. It can't be malaria, it must be sand-fly fever. As my book says, "This is endemic in the Maltese archipelago"!

After three days I feel a little better, but very weak. I drag myself up and just manage to start the Dodge which has been a bit unreliable recently, by running it down a slight slope outside the hotel. I drive up to the airfield.

What utter desolation! Not a soul about anywhere and here is this eerie ghost airfield, covered with black oil drums. There are a few figures moving about in the distance, scavenging.

I draw my service pistol (which I have never used) and put a couple of rounds into it and indulge in a bit of target practice on the oil drums. The result is instantaneous, all the scavengers disappear like magic.

With a great effort, I pack up all the medical supplies in a box or two, load them into my truck. Then down to Xlendi again and bed.

My hair is falling out and I feel very depressed.

For about a week I carry on like this, recovering slowly. I wander about the island in my truck. There is a nice beach down at Marsalforn, the other side of the island, and I go down there in the afternoons and lie on the shore and wish I had someone to talk to!

I really believe everyone has forgotten me. Presumably there is a battle going on in Sicily somewhere but I might just as well be on the moon, it is all so remote. I feel as if I'm living in a dream in the aftermath of this wretched fever.

At last a letter comes from RAF HQ in Malta. It is brought to me by an RAF corporal, in a jeep, which has come over specially. I gather he had some difficulty in finding me! Anyhow, the letter says to report back to Malta immediately.

Well, I don't mind if I do now! It does not take me long to pack my few belongings. We then strike the tent, which has been my surgery and general headquarters for about two months and pack it into the back of the Dodge truck. Then a hurried goodbye to mother superior and theatre sister in the little hospital. I think they are sorry to see me go after all our excitement.

A last look at the abandoned air strip and then we are off, down to the harbour where an old tank landing craft awaits us. It is full of odd bits and pieces of equipment and a lot of oil drums, full of fuel presumably. The jeep and my Dodge truck are the last on board. Soon Gozo is shimmering in the haze astern.

Dear Gozo, you never knew what hit you, did you? You already look like a dream island. I don't believe all this last two months' hectic activity disturbed you very much, although surely you must have noticed what was going on. Well, you can go back to sleep now, I am the last of your disturbers and invaders and I am already half way to Malta. Goodbye! I wonder if I shall ever see you again?

Epilogue

A fter the events recorded here, I went back to my old job at Hal Far, in Malta for a couple of months. The war had passed on and over Malta, and Hal Far was very quiet — almost a peace-time station. There was very little to do. I taught myself to sail, by going out most afternoons in a small rather over-canvassed boat in Kalafrana bay. There was an old dual-control Harvard Training aircraft on the station and I flew in this quite a lot with a very "browned-off" Fleet Air Arm pilot called David Langdon, who was left at Hal Far with a Fulmar (old-type Fleet Air Arm fighter aircraft). His function was to tow an air target round the island which was used for gunnery practice. He was indescribably bored by this; however he made a good companion, and he used to take me up in the Harvard and show me every aerobatic there was!

The redoubtable CO of the station, Wg Cdr Prosser-Hanks DFC, even tried to teach me to fly in the Harvard trainer. He was distinctly nervous after my first glide landing with him, and I was posted soon after! In September I made my way to 21 Mobile Field Hospital of the Desert Air Force in Italy at Foggia, as assistant surgeon. This was a satisfying and even reasonably busy job, as we followed close on the heels of the armies during the Italian campaign.

Then my last year overseas was spent at the RAF General Hospital Algiers, again as assistant surgeon.

I arrived home in a Liberator, this time *with* a parachute, in September 1945, after three years overseas service.

Then the business of making my way in my chosen

profession (surgery) engulfed me. There were exams to pass, and lots of work to be done.

There was the business of getting married, having children, and acquiring new responsibilities of every sort along the way. Eventually in 1954 I achieved my goal, being appointed consultant surgeon to St Thomas' Hospital, London in that year.

There followed a crowded and busy surgical life, which left little time for looking back over my shoulder, so to speak!

However the events of that amazing year I spent, as a very green young doctor, in Malta and Gozo remained very fresh at the back of my mind. Over the years, at odd times, as the fancy took me, I would jot down little reminiscences.

The story of Malta and Gozo was told to my wife and family and some friends, in bits and pieces, over many years, in private moments!

As the years went by these events receded into the far distance, and in fact after 45 years had gone by I began to wonder myself whether it had all actually happened. Perhaps it was really all a dream. Memory of far distant events does play funny tricks.

At last in 1987 my wife suggested that really we ought to go back to Malta on holiday, to see it all.

And so exactly 45 years later I found myself ascending that well-remembered track from Birzebuggia up to Hal Far airfield, this time in a hired car and with my wife by my side.

As we got to the top of the hill, I could scarcely believe my eyes as we entered the deserted gates of Hal Far, and the vista of the old airfield burst upon our eyes.

The incredible thing was that it was almost exactly as I had left it 45 years ago: but now it was a ghost airfield, dusty and untended, not a soul about. There was the runway on which so many memorable events had taken place. In a sort of flashback I saw Flt Lt Atkinson making that brilliant crash landing in his damaged Spitfire, all those years ago! We drove along it as fast as the car could manage!

There were even old remains of crashed aircraft about the place, and the old buildings round the parade ground and control tower were still there. They had all been renovated and patched up and were looking quite smart. True, there was a large new up-to-date control tower, a little way away from the deserted old concrete control building which I had known.

So, it hadn't all been a dream, it was all true, and memories came flooding over me so fast and furious I could scarcely contain them. On that day I knew I would have to write down some of the events of those days, as seen through my young and immature eyes, in order to get it out of my system.

Then we went to Gozo. There was absolutely no trace to be found of the old airstrip! But all over the island, in odd places, often serving bizarre functions were the old well-remembered oil drums. Some were used as parts of fences, others for storage, and so on. After a good deal of hunting and enquiries we found an old man who remembered the airfield, and told us exactly where it was. We found it at last, all ploughed up and returned to nature with vegetables growing in neat rows, and furrows in the rich red earth. I could have been forgiven for not spotting it, because at the end of the main runway, they had built an enormous cathedral. This church was built on the outskirts of the village of Xewkija, and was constructed entirely by the villagers themselves. It is an impressive monument to the skill of the Gozitan stone masons and to the religious spirit of the island. However, standing as it does, right on the end of the main runway of what was the old air-strip it certainly puts paid to any further use of this area for aircraft landings!

As I strolled over the fields, with my wife and son, I looked for the area where my old tented sick quarters had been, and after some doubt, I felt I had pinpointed the spot. Somehow I felt that my companions were not too impressed, as the whole area looked so peaceful with its rows of little fields and vegetable plantations. Everything looked so settled and permanent. It was very hard to imagine a full operational fighter airfield here!

And then it happened! A man, a local Gozitan, walked up to us as we stood in the middle of the fields, a rather incongruous little group.

He said, "I know what you are looking for. It's the old airfield, isn't it?"

Well, it turned out that he was a boy of about 12 when it all happened, and of course at that age it was all a great excitement for him. His memories of it were even sharper than mine. Yes, he said, the hospital(?) was over there: the ack-ack battery was there; the Spitfire pens were over there. He managed to bring the whole place alive in a few minutes.

I asked him if there was any monument or record to mark the spot. No, he said, most people have forgotten it altogether!

This indeed was only too evident. The whole area had returned to nature, and the whole episode was forgotten.

A little later we found the old hospital in Victoria. It is now a civic headquarters. My old operating theatre is now an office. The young clerks there were both amazed and amused when I recounted to them my surgical adventures in that very room.

Gozo is a very tranquil island. About three thousand years of visible history have rolled over it, without, I suspect, altering the life style of its inhabitants very much. So why should two months of activity in the latest of many Mediterranean wars be of any concern? Quite so!

All the same, it is nice that somebody should remember the events which took place on a quiet field of onions, cabbages and tomatoes near Xewkija, on Gozo.

APPENDIX 1

THE FLEET AIR ARM AT HAL FAR

The Fleet Air Arm being neither straight navy, nor RAF, but somewhere in between, often gets left out of the history books. Nowhere is this more true than in the history of the battle of Malta. The contribution of these pilots receives only passing mention in all the accounts that I have read.

However, in June 1943 an American war correspondent called Afred Wagg spent the week of 21–27 June with the navy pilots at Hal Far. (At the time I was in Gozo.) He was so impressed with what he saw and heard, that he wrote a long piece about them. This, typically, was never published at the time as other more interesting items took over the newspaper space.

But, later in 1943 he and a fellow journalist, David Brown, published a book of articles recording at first hand the events leading up to the invasion of Sicily and the early part of the Italian campaign. This book called *No spaghetti for breakfast* has long been out of print. In it he includes the piece he wrote about the Fleet Air Arm pilots of Hal Far. It is the best, and as far as I can discover, the only detailed "write up" of their achievements.

I reproduce here—verbatim—a part of it.

. . . In the course of the next few days I flew and lived with the boys of the Albacores. Unfortunately at the time the world was talking about other things, and the story received no attention.

The first line in my note-book read: "They take off, fly, land and crash at 70 miles per hour." "They" are a tiny squadron of Royal Navy pilots who, with their crews, fly old-fashioned bi-wing planes from the world's most bombed airfield in Malta, and they have hung up a new and astonishing record.

Because I believe that this record fits in with the heroism of the Mediterranean and the part it played in accomplishing the armistice with Italy, I am re-telling this story.

The Albacores, during their time in Malta, sank more Axis shipping in the Mediterranean than the total "kill" of any other Allied air force. From the inadequate cockpits of Albacores and Swordfish—more affectionately called "Stringbags"—they have managed to sink an average of one ship per fortnight for three long years. More than 75 Italian ships sunk are on the scoreboard in the squadron's mess. More than twice this number of enemy ships were damaged. And, after those three years, the boys were still fighting, still flying, still kings in their own right, proving to a lot of folks that flying classy new planes doesn't necessarily sink ships.

On looking back into the Albacores' past, Tunisia had proved to be a "heyday" for the Albacore pilots. In Tunisia the game was plentiful and there was no bag-limit. But there was no reward for the hunter, either! The navy fliers did their work behind the retreating armies' lines—"behind the scenes," in fact.

The sinking of Axis oil and gunpowder from the time of El Alamein onwards was equally as controlling an advantage over the enemy as the winning of battles in the desert. For it was the guys with the aerial torpedoes who went out each night "coast-crawling" right into the enemy harbours, sinking supplies that Rommel could not replace, from Trapani to Messina, who had weighted the scale in our favour. They flew on armed rover patrols day and night. While the "desert rats" were preparing to oust Rommel from Egypt, the Albacores were firing their "tin fish" into the convoys sailing from Italy to Benghazi, Tripoli and other Italian, German, and French ports.

The success that was theirs could not—by any stretch of the imagination—be accredited to their speed or their equipment. Rather, their success was entirely due to a new technique developed in the school of experience.

One pilot explained the method thus: "When we attack, we glide down noiselessly from several thousand feet towards our target. A few feet above the water we straighten out and, from a dead level position, fire our torpedo. Then we whip away—if we can!"

"If the position of the plane isn't exactly level, then the tin fish noses down and wastes itself in the water. If it hits fins first, then it generally goes careering off at an angle, diving and surfacing like a porpoise. When you can't see—and the weather's bleak and black—dropping torpedoes from our ancient planes isn't any fun."

As the tides of war began to turn and the Germans back-stepped to Tripoli, they were desperately in need of more material—oil, munitions, arms, tanks and trucks. It was about this time that the Germans and Italians really began to fear — believe it or not!— the accurate torpedoing of these slow-moving, cumbersome Albacores.

But the going really began to get rough about the time of the siege of Tripoli, when the enemy air-power in the Mediterranean was reinforced with Messerschmidt 109s, which came south from Italy and Sicity in swarms. It was about this time that the escorts provided by the Italians for the convoys began to increase. The introduction of new guns threw up flak that was an added hazard. The "bi-wing" boys had to fly right down close to the water, practically touching the crests of the white-caps, like seagulls, and the introduction of this new Italian gun—which depressed its angle of fire to almost a level position—was a new danger.

One young Scottish observer told me that coming down low like that over the water gives you the feeling that you are hiding in an ambush. "You almost feel," he said, "as if no one could see you." He went on to explain how important it was that one should feel that way, for when the ack-ack gunners started throwing up at you everything in the gun-barrels, there is little enough security anyhow. By going flat out, it is more difficult for the enemy to take aim. Even with new guns, which were depressible to the horizon level, a target which came in against an inky-sea background was difficult to hit.

Despite all the flak and the dangerous conditions in which these boys did their flying, they had comparatively few losses. Like the American Volunteer Group in China, their record stands as an air-epic in the air. In more than 12 000 operational flying hours over the Mediterranean, behind the enemy's lines, this squadron has had only 49 men missing and 11 taken prisoner. These figures represent 32 planes shot down over a period of three years, and include two crews which were rescued.

As Rommel fell back on Tripoli and Tunisia last winter, one of his chief worries was the shortage of oil. In response to his pleas, the Germans began to run ships down the Sicilian coast each night on a regular schedule, by-passing Malta on either side. The job remaining for the "stringbags" was quadrupled. Orders were obvious. Andrew Cunningham's orders were, "Sink and keep on sinking tankers". This order must have been an inspiration for that last order of Cunningham's when, at the end in Tunisia he said: "Sink, burn, or destroy, let nothing pass." So weeks before Cunningham had issued his history-making order, the Albacores were carrying out a "private" order along the same lines.

The tankers were heavily escorted. The job was not an easy one. Some of the boys didn't come back. But the Albacores sank so many tankers that the enemy's African effort was being crippled. Until then, the Albacores had carefully avoided any short-cut over Sicily. The hazard was enemy fighters. But it was becoming imperative to increase the Albacores' range along the Italian coast-line. So the risk was taken. Ack-ack over Sicily was well known and accurate. And the Albacores were not at their best in an operation across land. However, a large tanker was reported coming out of Naples, they simply could not resist having a go at topping Sicily in order to reach the target. It was in the middle of March this year, and that Rommel had intended that particular ship to arrive intact was obvious from the amount of escort present. Four of the "kites" took off—three came back, but the tanker was "properly pranged."

On the first leg of the trip across Sicily one of the planes crashed into a mountain. This was doubly unfortunate since it was carrying the flares which were to illuminate the target. A few minutes later the other three crews were jolted by an explosion of ack-ack fire from Palermo batteries, over which they had arrived in error. A mistake in navigation had brought them out in the wrong place. Happily, they only had a few holes punched in their fuselages. Ducking through the barrage, they flew along the coast, playing hide-and-seek in the cloud-banks partly obscuring the moon. The sea was inky-black and they flew only 5000 feet above the water, and stooged around trying to find their target. After many minutes of hunting, the convoy fired a few rounds, and so revealed its position. But unfortunately the few spurts of gun-fire did not provide sufficient light to determine the order of the convoy.

For some time they orbited the convoy's approximate position, waiting their chance to nip in. Realizing their presence was known, they expected a difficult time. Finally, the convoy appeared outlined in a half-moon path through a gap in the clouds. A sub-lieutenant in the Royal Navy (T. Barr, of Glasgow) dived down from the land side and, in true Albacore fashion, added the 7000-ton tanker to the mess-room's unique score-board.

One of the boys, sipping a double-gin-and-bitters from a white navy mug, summed up their troubles thus: The Albacore pilots had three major headaches. The first was to find that speck of a target on the broad Mediterranean, and to do this you had to "know your ships".

One pilot, flying at night, had sighted a convoy and dropped flares before he recognized that they were British destroyers! A few minutes later he sighted another group of ships which he could not identify, and, turning back, he led the British destroyers over towards the target. As a result, the destroyers sank one Italian ship and a large enemy ammunition ship.

The second headache was to get your tin fish into that most-times-difficult-to-see target. Lastly, but equally important, was to find your way home to a little cross on the map—Malta!

The night after Barr's strike, four Albacores went out on

an armed rover patrol along the north-western coast of Sicily. "Fingers" Lewis (who in training school had been dubbed "the dunce") made his maiden operational flight and bagged a 6000-ton ammunition ship en route for North Africa. He had found his target just off Marittimo. The ship was in company with two smaller merchantmen and their escorting destroyers. He flew between the two destroyers and into point-blank range firing his tin fish. An explosive shell burst behind his cockpit, but "Fingers" was able to get home.

The boys claimed that they were the first to give the Italians a super-case of the jitters. With the "help" of their mascot, a small penguin toy doll, they had emerged from the blitz "victors" in anybody's language! The doll, however, had ironically written across it their motto: "Get me outta here."

APPENDIX 2

"Operation Gozo"

The following is the account of the construction of Gozo's airstrip in 1943, taken from the official record of the battle of Malta—"Malta Blitzed, But Not Beaten" by Philip Vella, (1985).

～～～～～～～～～～～～～～

The underground War Headquarters at Lascaris was a beehive of activity as British and American officials worked on the plans for the operation, code-named "Husky" (Sicily invasion). Aerial support was of paramount importance and the need was felt for further reinforcements to General George Patton's Seventh Army during and after the initial stages of the assault.

Since airfields and dispersal areas in Malta could not take the additional Spitfires required for this purpose, it was decided to build an airfield at Gozo. A strip of cultivated land skirting the villages of Xewkija, Ghajnsielem, Nadur and Xagra was chosen. Lord Gort requested Bishop Gonzi to approach the farmers, who agreed to cede their fertile fields against adequate compensation.

Construction was assigned to the Americans. Company "E" 2nd Battalion, 21st Engineer Aviation Regiment left Sousse in Tunisia on the 1st June 1943, on nine landing craft tanks. The convoy, carrying six officers and one hundred and ninety-seven men, and their equipment, reached Marsalforn Bay on the 6th June. Work on an east–west runway started two days later. Tractors, scrapers and mechanical shovels levelled the area: the historic Gourgion Tower, which stood in the way, had to be demolished. The American servicemen and Gozitan labourers worked in earnest with two shifts operating from 0500 to 2100 hours.

When Sir Keith Park visited the site some days later, he ordered the construction of an additional runway as well as revetments or blast pens. Additional equipment and seventy thousand sand bags were shipped from Malta; this required the setting up of three shifts working twenty-four hours a day. Work on the second runway started on 15th June with about 300 Gozitans constructing revetments of stone and sand bags.

Both runways, each measuring 150 feet by 4,000 feet, were completed on 20th June, while work continued on the construction of taxiways, hardstandings and revetments. The new dispersal facilities provided accommodation for seventy-eight aircraft.

The airstrips became operational on 22nd June 1943, and the first American-piloted Spitfires of 31st Fighter Group landed on the following day.

Work on the airfield was completed on 25th June and five days later Company "E" returned to North Africa. The British authorities had doubts whether the work could be completed in time: in fact it was ready one week ahead of schedule. This was made possible by the efficiency of American engineers, who had at their disposal the most modern mechanical equipment existing at the time, the labour of Gozitan workers and the persuasive manner of Mgr Gonzi who, soon afterwards, became Malta's Archbishop and was subsequently created a Knight of the British Empire in recognition of his services to the Allied cause.

‌

APPENDIX 3

WING CO. ADRIAN WARBURTON—P.R.U. PILOT EXTRAORDINARY!

"Wing Commander A. Warburton," says an official history of the air battle of Malta, "first came to the island at the end of 1940, and specialized in reconnaissance flying, with only short interruption, throughout the period covered in these pages (the whole of the siege)." His friend A. J. Spooner, the captain of a Wellington operating from Malta who knew him from early days, describes how

. . . in Egypt (he) borrowed a Beaufighter, stripped it of all armour plate guns, ammunition etc, installed vertical cameras and flew it to Malta. He dismissed the Baltimore (the official reconnaissance plane) with a wrinkle of his disdainful nose. "No bloody good. But this Beau," he said, "is the fastest aircraft in the Mediterranean. . . . With this I can reconnoitre any place at any time at any height." He photographed the Italian fleet in their naval base of Taranto in appalling weather from less than a hundred feet. He navigated himself all over the Mediterranean—without adequate meterorological services or navigational equipment. He went when they expected him and when they did not. He always came home undamaged, often followed by an armada of enemy fighters. He carried no guns or armour. He refused to fly with regular aircrew. He chose to fly with AC2 Haddon and LAC

Shirley, their role on board being to change the camera spools and to count aloud the enemy fighters following him. He liked to take his coat off and assist in servicing his own engines—a task for which he was not qualified. He would fly in almost any clothes provided they were not the official ones. A thigh-length pair of sheepskin leggings which he had acquired in Crete were characteristic. Above this he would wear army battledress with air-force stripes (he was now an acting flight lieutenant). He preferred an Ascot cravat to a tie. He was proud of his ash-blonde hair, so let it grow to near shoulder length. He had a notoriously grease-stained cap which he used to wear at times—on top of his flying helmet even. Against orders he smoked as he flew. He would take little part in mess life at Luqa, but instead could be found on occasions playing cards with the airmen at the dispersal site in one of the homemade huts there. Yet on one occasion, at a time when most of us had run out of buttons, polish and smart uniforms, he turned up in the mess immaculately dressed in order to meet the new group captain. He was like that—utterly unpredictable. He lived in Valletta with a charming cabaret artiste, and he drove himself to work in an old car. . . . Although not by nature a normally contented person, I believe that he found himself—and happiness—in Malta. And later, when posted to other Mediterranean bases, he found unofficial ways of returning to the island that welcomed him an appreciated him."

The Air Battle of Malta (HMSO 1944) has the following anecdote. "While carrying out, unarmed, a low-level photographic reconnaissance of Bizerta in November 1942, Warburton was attacked and shot up by Me 109s. His aircraft was hit in the engine, oil tank and compass, and he was compelled to land at Bone. He made his way, via Algiers, to Gibraltar, where he collected a fighter (a Spitfire) which was awaiting delivery to Malta. While flying this machine back he encountered two Ju 88s in the Gulf of Tunis and attacked them. One he shot down, the other managed to escape into cloud. He then returned to his astonished colleagues who had already given him up as missing, having heard nothing of him for four days." Later in the war Warburton was "loaned" to the USAF for photographic missions after the big USAF daylight raids over Europe. In the course of his air force career he had earned two Distinguished Service Orders, and three Distinguished Flying Crosses. He disappeared finally under mysterious circumstances and it is right that his friend Group Captain Spooner should have the last word: "Needless to say, he was flying an aircraft (an American one) that didn't belong to him . . . Some profess to believe that he is still alive. Just as some believe that Laurence of Arabia still lives. With such men, and there was much in common between them, anything is possible—anything other than the ordinary." This and the quotation in text are from A. Spooner, *In Full Flight* (Macdonald, 1965).

Sources of illustrations

I am grateful to the Imperial War Museum for permission to reproduce the eight photographs (Figure 3 to 10 inclusive) in this book. All other photographs (except Figure 1) were taken by my wife — Dorothea. The perpetrator of Figure 1 is unknown.